Praise for Lesley Garner's books:

'This follow up to her Everything I've Ever Done That Worked *is as refreshingly down-to-earth and nourishing in its wisdom as its predecessor.'*

The Bookseller

'deeply honest … Lesley Garner's experience is gleaned from her own experience.'

The Times

This beautiful book looks at love in all aspects… The effect is to bathe you in softness and wisdom.'

Health and Fitness magazine

'For thirty years I have admired Lesley Garner as a writer. This book is a huge celebration of life and how we can, in simple ways, enrich our days. A wonderfully lyrical work … I recommend it to anyone who wants to feel happier, more fulfilled and increasingly to enjoy the world around them.'

Jilly Cooper

'Lesley Garner is one of those remarkable women who is original, full of insights and common sense, while writing with a sparkle and fluency that is envied by her peers and hugely enjoyed by her many admirers.'

Sir Max Hastings

'A priceless collection of reflections, observations and signposts towards a happier and more harmonious life. Wise, practical, elegant, inspiring and genuinely helpful.'

Mick Brown, author of *The Spiritual Tourist*

'A beautiful collection of short essays which act as a spiritual and emotional first-aid kit. Practical, insightful and moving, this book is a perfect gift anyone looking for inspiration.'

The Guardian

'Lesley Garner has produced the perfect bedside book for those nights when you can't sleep and it's too late to call a friend ... An inspiring and elegantly written companion.'

You magazine

'Superb.'

The Independent

'I never put down Everything I've Ever Done That Worked *without gleaning some sort of solace or inspiration.'*

The Saturday Times magazine

'I tried to ration myself to a chapter a night but on the fifth night I gave in and gobbled it up. For such an important book it is quite fascinating and very easy to read. I am sure it will help many people as it has helped me.'

Shirley Conran

Everything I've Ever Learned About Love

Everything I've Ever Learned About Love

Lesley Garner

HAY HOUSE
Australia • Canada • Hong Kong
South Africa • United Kingdom • United States

First published and distributed in the United Kingdom by:
Hay House UK Ltd, 292B Kensal Rd, London W10 5BE. Tel.: (44) 20 8962 1230; Fax: (44) 20 8962 1239.
www.hayhouse.co.uk

Published and distributed in the United States of America by:
Hay House, Inc., PO Box 5100, Carlsbad, CA 92018-5100. Tel.: (1) 760 431 7695 or (800) 654 5126; Fax (1) 760 431 6948 or
(800) 650 5115. www.hayhouse.com

Published and distributed in Australia by:
Hay House Australia Ltd, 18/36 Ralph St, Alexandria NSW 2015. Tel.: (61) 2 9669 4299; Fax: (61) 2 9669 4144.
www.hayhouse.com.au

Published and distributed in the Republic of South Africa by:
Hay House SA (Pty), Ltd, PO Box 990, Witkoppen 2068. Tel./Fax: (27) 11 706 6612. orders@psdprom.co.za

Published and distributed in India by:
Hay House Publishers India, Muskaan Complex, Plot No.3, B-2, Vasant Kunj, New Delhi - 110 070.
Tel.: (91) 11 41761620; Fax: (91) 11 41761630. contact@hayhouseindia.co.in

Distributed in Canada by:
Raincoast, 9050 Shaughnessy St, Vancouver, BC V6P 6E5. Tel.: (1) 604 323 7100; Fax: (1) 604 323 2600

Cover and interior design: Leanne Siu

The moral rights of the author have been asserted.

The author of this book does not dispense medical advice or prescribe the use of any technique as a form of treatment
for physical or medical problems without the advice of a physician, either directly or indirectly. The intent of the
author is only to offer information of a general nature to help you in your quest for emotional and spiritual well-being.
In the event you use any of the information in this book for yourself, which is your constitutional right, the author and
the publisher assume no responsibility for your actions.

A catalogue record for this book is available from the British Library.

ISBN 978-1-4019-0544-6 (HB)
ISBN 978-1-4019-1529-2 (PB)

Printed and bound in Europe for Imago.

For my mother and father,
who taught me by example

Contents

Introduction

Love has six billion faces. That is how many people there are in the world, although there will be more by the time you finish reading this paragraph. Actually, love has more than six billion faces because each human being has many faces of love. The loving face I turn towards my mother is subtly different from the face I turn towards my lover or my child, and different still from the loving face I turn towards a landscape or my home or a favourite painting. And love has billions of faces beyond that: the faces of the ancestors stretching back millions of years into the past. Cro-Magnon woman knew love as she held her baby. The first cave artists knew love as they swept the line of a bison on to the cave wall and left their handprints beside it.

What I am trying to say is that love is a force with infinite expressions. With each page that I have written, I have become more aware of my own limitations in trying to filter this infinite experience through one finite life and sensibility. I am a single human being, stuck in time and place, with many limitations, and yet I am writing a book that claims to be everything I have ever learned about love, in the hope that I might have some insights to pass on to you. Somewhere between the infinite manifestations of love and my single human existence I hope that I have stumbled across some universal experiences. Before you read on I want you to take certain things into account.

One is that I am a woman and, although I have tried to see love from all sides, I have inevitably written from a woman's perspective. If that leaves male readers feeling misunderstood I apologise. Please tell me what I've got wrong and help me understand you better.

Another thing is that I am British. On the list of nationalities with a reputation for emotional warmth, ease with our bodies and spontaneity with our hearts, the British don't come high. We are often embarrassed when it comes to love, and private, except under the influence of alcohol when we embarrass everybody else. We don't have the American ease with declaring our feelings, and we have none of the *savoir-faire* of the French or passion of the Italians. So, on the subject of love, I've had to work out a few things from first principles.

I am single, at the time of writing. I am not in love or in a relationship with anybody, although I have been married and I have children and I have had many relationships in my life. My single state bothered me while I was writing this book, but it had its advantages too. It gave me a calm perspective to look at the hurly-burly. Wordsworth said that poetry came from emotion recollected in tranquillity. A lot of this book comes from the same source.

I am in mid life. I think this is a big advantage for somebody writing about love. I inhabit a body that carries the recollection and the possibility of passion, but is free of the constant turmoil of hormonal tides. With my head above these emotional waters, I am far more aware than I used to be of the infinite ways in which love manifests in our lives. I value friendship almost more highly than passion. I am old enough to be aware of the poignancy and tenderness of my relationship with my ageing parents. I am aware of the constant shifts in my relationship with my growing daughters. The greatest lessons in love are in our dealings with the people who are attached to us throughout life, because there is never any question of giving up. This is why marriage, the committed lifelong relationship, is still the most powerful crucible for human love.

I have an aim in writing this book, which is to remind people that love isn't just about romantic couples, and it is certainly not just about sexual passion. If anyone takes anything valuable from this book I hope that, apart from understanding how to negotiate human relationships with more kindness, skill and patience, it is that the sources of love are manifold.

Romantic love hogs all the headlines, but if people look honestly at their lives they may find that the solace and courage, the challenge and fulfilment, the unforgettable moments haven't all come from being in a couple at all. Freud said that the healthy person should be able to function in love and work. Sometimes love and work are indivisible. If a good fairy appeared at my child's cradle and offered the gift of happiness in love or happiness in a life's work, it would be a hard choice. It is glorious to get up in the morning excited about what you are going to do that day. It is a wonderful thing to think, "I love my job." It is a wonderful thing to engage with and have an impact on the wider world. And it is wonderful to love where we live, to love our homes, to love a landscape, to love a favourite book, film or song, to love running or sailing or climbing.

If I could say one thing to someone young, it would be: don't fixate on finding your one true love. Remember to explore your passions.

Whatever they are they will lead you to the person you were designed to be. Of course life is richer if you share it with one special person, but it is not the only way to be. Enthusiasm is another divine face of love. It is part of love's definition.

And what is love behind its infinite faces? I hope the rest of this book gives you many answers, but the more I consider it, the more I see love as the prime gravitational force in human lives. Whether it is biological, emotional or spiritual, love is the force that draws us to one another and binds us together into a whole that is more than the sum of its parts. It is the search for completeness that gives meaning to our lives, and without a sense of meaning we are on the road to despair. We are born separate, and love is the force that drives and draws us to wholeness. Whether love shows its face to you through human relationships, art, science, politics or contact with nature, I believe it is looking for you as much as you are looking for it.

Trailing Clouds of Glory

Love is mystery, and so the state of wonder is the first face of love. It is a face of wide-eyed, open-mouthed, breath-held, heart-stopped innocence. It is a wordless state, a pause before language forms. It is the state that occupies the boundlessness of love. It is the egoless state. When it hits you, the armies of little fears and vanities, plans and memories that make up the ego retreat, and the heart is left exposed and open to what is before it. The heart sees. In adult life, with another human being before our eyes, this might be the hit of love at first sight. In a child, it is the state that marks a new meeting with the world. It can be triggered by a butterfly, a leaf or a trick of the light. Some people never lose the right of entry into the state of wonder, and their lives are blessed.

The writer Gwen Raverat, in her memoir *Period Piece*, describes it perfectly when she writes about her childhood visits to Down, the country home of her grandfather, Charles Darwin. She describes the sea-pebbles embedded in the garden path:

"I adored those pebbles. I mean literally, adored; worshipped. This passion made me feel quite sick sometimes. And it was adoration that I felt for the foxgloves at Down, and for the stiff red clay out of the Sandwalk clay pit; and for the beautiful white paint on the nursery floor. This kind of feeling hits you in the stomach and in the ends of your fingers, and it is probably the most important thing in life. Long after I have forgotten all my human loves, I shall still remember the smell of a gooseberry leaf or the feel of the wet grass on my bare feet; or the pebbles in the path. In the long run it is this feeling that makes life worth living, this which is the driving force behind the artist's urge to create."

When I think about the state of wondering in-loveness I was in as a child, I immediately find myself back in my own grandfather's garden in south Wales. I see myself down among the cabbages, absorbed by a raindrop caught on a leathery blue-green leaf. I can feel the softness of the thick daisy-strewn grass under the lilac tree. I remember the intense sense of mystery and loss of scale as I gazed into the dark, moss-lined subterranean world revealed by the removal of a large stone in the vegetable patch.

The loving act of looking, which I began by gazing into my mother's face, was transferred to the whole new world. I loved the grain of wood on my grandmother's old oak dresser. I loved the green pressed-glass bowls which she used to serve rhubarb and custard. The oak dresser now stands in my own kitchen, and I cried when it arrived because it brought my grandmother's essence with it. I still can't resist green pressed glass.

I loved going to the nearby beaches and exploring on the rocks, hanging my head over the clear water of the rock pools to see the magic world inside, pushing my finger into the red velvet mouths of sea anemones to feel their adhesive little tentacles cling to my fingertip. Love absorbed me. Absorption is a sign of love throughout life. Where you see a human being happily absorbed in an activity, a view, a piece of music, another human being, you are looking at a manifestation of love.

When does the wonder, the absorption, the magical connection with the world vanish? It does vanish slowly for everyone who doesn't consciously cultivate it in adulthood. When does the spell break?

I think it breaks with growing self-consciousness. We literally get in our own way. Somebody might laugh at us for being dreamy and that is the end of our dreaming. Tasks and targets and duties and desires block our innocent connection with the world around us. In the words of William Wordsworth, who knew: "shades of the prison house begin to close about the growing boy." We individualise. The question "Who am I?" begins to be more important than "What is that?" It replaces the primal ecstatic state that simply receives and asks no questions at all.

The danger is of falling out of love with the world. The danger is of leaving the state of wonder for the fallen state of separation. The feeling of separation is so terrifying that we scan the faces around us to see who will rescue us. Our hormones and the sexual drive focus all our energies on finding our union with life through the narrow gateway of one other person, the One.

The good news is that the lost paradise is always there waiting for us. One way to re-enter it is simply to pay extreme attention to what is around us. Another way to rediscover it is to travel somewhere new. The dust of blinding familiarity hasn't settled on a strange landscape. Our mind doesn't gloss over it, unseeing, saying, "Been there, know that". Strangeness will wake us up again because, for our very survival, we have to pay close attention to it.

I travelled to Ethiopia once for a two-week holiday trip. Two years later I found myself actually living there, but my senses were so open to its strangeness in that first trip that I never over-rode my first powerful impressions: the white-robed horsemen riding scarlet-caparisoned mules on the edge of great mountain gorges, the white lilies growing in the field under a stormy sky, the evening smoke rising through the thatch of the village huts, the great lammergeyers riding the thermals. First I saw with the eyes of a child and I wondered. Later, when I was living there, I thought I knew what I was looking at, and that stopped me seeing. This deadening process of familiarity happens in relationships too.

It is much harder to capture the first magic of a relationship because so much habit and emotion have got in the way, but the pebbles in the path and the raindrop on the cabbage leaf are always waiting for us to take the time to see them. Many of the struggles and continual dissatisfied yearning of adult life arise partly because nothing can permanently fill the gap left by our loss of connection with life itself. It is very unreasonable of us to expect one human being to stand in for the whole universe. Hard as it is, it is important to stop whenever and wherever we can and try to see through the eyes of a child.

Greeting Ben

Ben is the first baby to be born to my children's generation of the family. He has turned my sister and brother-in-law into grandparents, and made an aunt and uncle out of his mother's brother and sister. He is the first real baby that my own daughters, his cousins, have got to observe at close quarters, the first real baby they've got to hold and gaze and marvel at.

Everyone has the same expression on their faces as they approach brand new Ben, and Ben had better make the most of it because this unguarded astonishment and approval won't last forever. But for the moment Ben's sky is full of human suns. They beam down on him, their eyes wide open and shining, their mouths wide open and smiling and exclaiming with delight. Ben's new world is a little solar system held together with the gravity of joy. He sees nothing but love and wonder. He sees the expressions human beings have when they behold the marvellous. The faces, all glowing and open, tell him that he is miraculous, adorable, delicious. My own face is as illuminated by pleasure as all the rest.

When I observe Ben's family greeting Ben into the world, I think how lucky Ben is to be illuminated with such love. And I think how lucky we are to be given this fresh start, this new human being to practise our loving on. The miracle is compounded when, a few weeks on, Ben smiles back. Entranced by this responsiveness, this clear communication, we all beam all the harder. There are six, seven, eight of us in the room, all focusing our solar power on Ben. How can he not bloom and grow and reflect all this loving energy right back at us? And he is changing us too.

Thanks to Ben we have a new focus. The relationships between everyone in the room are subtly changed as they adopt new roles. Some of this we joyfully share, and some of it is private. I know that everyone in this family has their own thoughts about babies and about the roles they each want to play in each other's lives. Ben is a little shock wave at the heart of his young parents' relationship, but the ripples move through all of us.

Ben is not unique. This is how it is with babies if they are lucky. Love is attention and, if babies are to trust the world and stay sunny, they need all this good attention beamed at them. Above all, they need it in order to feel and express their own love. Ben's growing brain is getting the habit of happiness. In a happy family this essential attention is given to babies with unconscious, unmeasured generosity. We can't help ourselves from greeting Ben with all the love at our disposal, because that is how we were greeted when it was our turn to be new.

Watching Ben glowing in this solar heat of the heart makes me think about other babies, millions of them, who are not greeted this way – babies who are unwanted, abandoned, starved, abused. How can they grow without this palpable encouragement? Even Ben's little brother or sister, one day, will not get quite this much undivided attention, because there will already be Ben. And Ben will have to cope with the shocking experience of seeing all these people who love him show the same love to somebody even smaller and newer than he is. How will Ben cope with the normal but awful realisation that his place in the sun must be shared?

And I think about us – adults sharing the renewing power of a baby. Some months later we are all together on a family holiday in Scotland, and it is newly special because we have Ben. The house itself feels more purposeful because it shelters a baby. We have the excitement of Ben's first beach and Ben's first sandcastle. Ben gets his first chocolate Easter egg and he has gifts for us too. He gives us wonder, humour, innocence. He gives us the invigorating sense of life renewing itself and now rolling forward like a wave into the future. He gives us a lot to look forward to. And this is the heart of the exchange: that while we give him the love he needs to flourish and grow, he gives us the love that renews our reason for living.

The Look of Love

Love begins with the gaze, and it's over when you can no longer meet each other's eyes. This rule works for lovers, but the gaze starts much earlier than that. The first gaze, the one you can't remember, happened to you when you first came into the world. That was the gaze you gave and received, the longest, deepest emotional exploration of your life: the gaze you shared with your mother.

Before I became a mother myself nobody warned me what would happen. I sat in my hospital bed, propped up with pillows, my knees up and, laid on my thighs, a fat little Buddha swaddled in white shawls. The eyes of this first baby were a shock: dark, indeterminate, seeing and not seeing, not quite focused and yet seeming to take the whole world in. I gazed into those eyes quite unselfconsciously and they gazed back at me for what felt like weeks. I didn't know it, but I was being dictated to by my biological self. In gazing this intently at this new person in my life I was stimulating the production of oxytocin, the bonding hormone that triggers the benevolent emotions of love. "If Cupid's arrows are dipped in anything," says Dr Frank Tallis in his book *Love Sick*, "they are dipped in oxytocin." In mothers and lovers, oxytocin produces the softer feelings of affection, tenderness and warmth. If anything disturbs this hormonal process, such as separation or postnatal depression, mothers and babies can have serious difficulties in relating to each other. But I didn't know the theory. I was just doing what came naturally.

I found myself thinking how curious it was that there was no self-consciousness, no awkwardness about this intense, prolonged mutual gaze. I realised that in normal adult life it is very difficult to sustain a long silent look into someone else's eyes. Some people who have difficulty relating to other people find it impossible, and this impossibility is a signal of bigger problems.

And yet, when two people are falling in love, they also find themselves lost in this pointless, wordless gaze. What do you see when you look into somebody else's eyes? You see the eye itself: the white, the iris, the pupil. It is just a surface, but it doesn't feel like that. When someone looks into your eyes it feels as though they have caught you naked. It feels as though they can read and record your thoughts. It feels as though they have penetrated all the armour and defence created by the ego and have tunnelled to some secret soft centre.

Practised seducers know this. Monica Lewinsky claimed that President Clinton did it to her. "He just sort of looks at you," she said afterwards, "and he locks eyes with you and sort of peels away the layers of your being with his eyes and with his spirit and it's very intense."

Where there is no love, a direct gaze can be very threatening, an evil eye, a signal of aggression. But whether you react by opening up or by protecting yourself, you know that a direct gaze is an act of great significance.

The baby and the mother need to share this gaze. It is part of the bonding between them that ensures the baby's survival. And there is something of this sense of searching for trust, of the need for a deep knowing, that is behind the gaze of new lovers. Can I trust this person with my life? Who are they, really, behind the mask?

Mother and baby come at the gaze from the opposite direction to the lovers. Mother and baby are not separate beings in the early days. The process of separation and individuation hasn't really begun. They look in order to make a new territory out of a part of themselves. Lovers look in order to unite.

The days of the gaze won't last forever in either case. As a child grows they look outwards, and if you can get an adolescent to look you in the eye you're lucky. The adolescent has a hard enough job looking the world in the eye, let alone a penetrating parent. As for lovers, the way they look at each other says everything. I watched the body language of a young couple on a train recently. Her shoulders were turned against him, her gaze was fixed on the distance in an aggressive act of detachment. He was drawn to look at her, but the more he turned to her the more she turned away. The gaze, and the relationship, was visibly broken. When someone you love fails to meet your eyes you know that, at that moment, love is absent.

So this is a sign of love. It begins with eye contact with a stranger. Then there is the quick second look, the held gaze. There is a connection. And there is the period of bonding when you could drown in each other's eyes. If neither of you can look away something important is happening.

And if you can't quite meet their eye then the relationship is in trouble. The days of the gaze may be over.

The Power of Yearning

When I was a little girl, very secure and much loved, I was sometimes swept with an inexplicable sense of loss and longing. I felt it in the centre of my body like a sudden disturbing void. I can think myself backwards now and find myself in my bedroom with its view of London chimneypots. I am wearing my blue-and-white check school frock. Maybe I am six, seven, eight. I expect my mother is securely in the kitchen preparing lunch or tea. The day is sunny. I am playing happily by myself then, wham, this internal gulf opens up.

It is intense, physical and emotional, and it is quite without explanation. I can't understand it at all. What or who am I missing? What have I lost? Where is it I need to be? I had no answers to these questions, and as I scanned my world for some reason for the ache and disturbance they went, cleared like a summer storm, and I didn't have to think about them any more.

These moments of sourceless longing were rare, and I remember a time in my adult life when I felt secure and I hadn't had the feeling for a very long time. I tried to explain it to my mother then, this feeling of loss, of not belonging, that I experienced most intensely as a child.

And she said, rather tartly: "So you think you're a changeling, do you, that you belong to another family?" Oops. No, that wasn't it at all. The feeling wasn't that personal. It was much bigger, more like being stranded in the wrong place listening for some guiding signal home.

I think it was, and sometimes still is on the very rare occasions when it returns, nostalgia. The seafaring, wandering Greeks knew about nostalgia, a word made from their words *nostos*, 'homecoming', and *algos*, 'pain'. The pain of homecoming – or the pain of being separated from home.

We have overused the word and debased its power. We think nostalgia is reminiscing about the good old days, a fond look back at the silly clothes we used to wear, a dog we used to own, or the shop where we bought sweets on the way to school, or even the school, with its dusty milky gassy smells. Centuries of usage have reduced the elemental force of nostalgia to a branch of sentimentality, but there is nothing fond or soppy about nostalgia. It is a deep unbearable longing for home, for elsewhere, for that which is lost and without which, suddenly, we can hardly breathe.

If love is union, then nostalgia is the primal pain of separation on a cosmic scale. It is universal homesickness. I used to suffer badly from homesickness as a child, even as a teenager. I spent a whole holiday in France as a fifteen-year-old, my first trip abroad, looking at the rooftops of Paris and the pine-scented hills of Provence through a film of tears. I missed my parents. I missed my landscape. I spent my afternoon siestas reading the most English of poems, like Edward Thomas's "Adlestrop", time-travelling my way out of the meridional heat into the moist green English landscape.

A friend of my French family suddenly produced, for everyone's entertainment, a puzzling pot of English lemon curd, and I was quite undone by the label which told us that the lemon curd came from Winchcombe in Gloucestershire. Now I had never been to Winchcombe in my life but, in the cicada-vibrating brilliance of a Provencal afternoon, I was suddenly transported to the buttercup-dusted English meadows, looking down at a cluster of stone houses and a church tower, and there were my homesick tears again.

Perversely, six weeks later, because France had now worked its way into my heart despite my homesickness, there I was, looking out at the English countryside through the same tears, dreaming of the Mediterranean and the new French boyfriend I'd left behind, and wishing damply I was in France. Maybe a fifteen-year-old girl is just a siphon of tears looking for a place to flood.

Nostalgia, real nostalgia, is a much bigger deeper feeling than that. It is a feeling of loss for something huge, like a country or a state of grace. I am half Celt and Celts are really good at it, our music and poetry driven by it. Exile intensifies it and alcohol fuels it, which is why the bars of the world fill up with drunken Irish, Welsh and Scots mourning their lost mountains and moorlands. When I was newly married my young Scottish husband used to madden me, in late-night maudlin mode, by crooning, "Ay, it's a sad day I left the croft." To which the unsentimental answer is, "Why don't you go back there then?"

But real nostalgia is still bigger than that. It is a love for a place or a state to which you can never return; for first love, for childhood, for the Garden of Eden. At its most painful and inexplicable, as I felt it as a child, it is a love of and a deep longing for a place you can't even identify, and which you are afraid you will never find. In the years when I was happily married and was creating a family of my own I never felt it once.

I think this nostalgia is a universal feeling. The Welsh call it *hiraeth*, the Portuguese, *saudade*. It is part of the irresistible drive that urges us towards love with another in the unconscious belief that, by belonging to the One, we will no longer suffer this sense of cosmic exile. Personal love is the opiate that dulls the pain of the displaced human condition.

There are other ways of dealing with this sense of inner exile and emotional rootlessness. Music and art and poetry express these feelings, and drama connects us with others in a collective catharsis. Time spent in nature invariably reconnects me. I can feel lost on a street but not in a wood. Drugs – socially acceptable, legal or illegal, or prescribed like Prozac – dull the anxiety of isolation and loss, but leave us more devastatingly stranded when the effect wears off. Religion and spirituality offer many paths to explore our connections to one another and to the source of life that some call God. The supreme mystical religious experience is the loss of personal boundary and the sense of union with all life. Where there is union or the sense of it there is no nostalgia, because we have found our way home.

I had moments as a child when I knew that too. There were moments – on a beach, in a garden, up a tree – when I knew that I was part of a whole, not separate from the branch, the grass, the birds and the waves, and it made me intensely light and happy. Writing this and remembering, I realise for the first time that a child who felt that joined-up with the world, and knew the joy of that state, would naturally suffer an intense sense of loss when she was out of it. But not seeing these feelings as part of a natural continuum of love and connection as I can now, it is no wonder that child was so baffled by the existential pain, no wonder she was so relieved when the moment of nostalgia passed.

I was in my forties when I read William Wordsworth's "Ode on Intimations of Immortality" and realised what I had known, and that he had known it too:

Whither is fled the visionary gleam?
Where is it now, the glory and the dream?

Our birth is but a sleep and a forgetting:
The Soul that rises with us, our life's Star,
Hath had elsewhere its setting,
And cometh from afar.

Who knows where the home of the soul is, or even if we have one? I do know that there is one deep reverberating note on love's keyboard that is too low to be heard in the daily chatter. Sometimes, though, it catches us unawares and demands that we tune in. And for that moment, as we vibrate to it, we suffer from nostalgia, the eternal pain of no return.

Being Ill

I loved being ill as a child. When I was ill my mother's love for me was expressed in exquisitely detailed attention to my comfort and wellbeing. To be ill and in need of care was to open a delicious and rare vein of maternal love.

My mother was a bright spark of vibrant energy, but my illness dimmed her lamp to a comforting, embracing glow. It would begin with a thermometer placed under my tongue and the happy discovery that I really did have a temperature. After the crucial decision that I wasn't well enough to go to school (hooray), the most glorious rituals were set in place.

My pillows would be plumped up, and I would have what little breakfast I could eat on a tray in bed. Then the tray would be taken away and I would be wrapped up in a shawl and propped in a chair, while my mother swept any crumbs from the sheets and re-made my bed to an irresistible smoothness and placed a fresh hot-water bottle between the covers. I can still feel the bliss of climbing back in, the comforting fineness of the freshly piled stack of pillows, the cool unwrinkled smoothness of the sheets, the glorious warmth of the hot-water bottle. And then the covers would be drawn back over me. I would be tucked in firmly. A steaming hot mug of hot water, honey and squeezed lemon would be set on the bedside table.

I would surrender to this wonderful comfort, the solid manifestation of my mother's loving care. Is this why I love hotels? Because climbing into a freshly made bed, made by someone else with clean ironed sheets, plugs straight into my bodily memories of my mother's care of me?

When I became a mother, I practised the art of babying my children, and I recognise the satisfaction it gave my mother to behave this way. When someone you love is vulnerable there is a covert satisfaction in knowing that, for this while, they are also under your control. I loved the experience of knowing that my mother had to slow down to look after me. She, and I in my turn, probably loved the experience of having children slowed down long enough to return to the control and care of babyhood. Neither of us would have felt the same if it had gone on too long, and the love would have been contaminated with fear and anxiety if I had been seriously ill. Nevertheless, this was and is one of the more satisfying manifestations of love. Very nice the red roses and champagne. How lovely the surprise present or the romance of a good restaurant. But true love, in my mind and heart, is always expressed by a freshly made bed, and its invitation to complete surrender to someone else's loving care.

In the Arms of a Book

I can't remember when I learned to read, so I was too young to know that I had already met one of the loves of my life. There's a photograph of me at five or six, curled up in a deckchair under my grandfather's lilac tree, weighted down by a fascinating volume of the *Children's Encyclopaedia*. There's another photograph of me, aged seven or eight, curled up by the fireside under another book, while my mother reads in the other chair.

I know what the books are in the bookcase behind me in this photograph because I looked at them so many times. There's the *Collected Works of William Shakespeare* on their tissue-thin pages. There's my mother's condensed *History of Art*, whose reproductions were the beginnings of my love of art. There are the three hardbacks that make up *The Lord of the Rings* trilogy, one of them a first edition because my father and I were in such a hunger to read it as soon as it came out. They were my companions, my family, my friends.

When didn't I love books? When didn't I have a physical, emotional response to the smell, the gloss and the weight of a new book in its wrapper? I can feel the solidity of the *Nonsense Omnibus* of Edward

Lear as I handed over my Christmas book token. My stomach remembers the excitement of the yellow-wrapped copy of *Bambi* by Felix Salten that I got as an essay prize. I can recall the library stacks in every library I've ever entered. I can scan them for fairy tales and school stories, ballet books and theatre memoirs, grown-up novels and histories. I was like a little horse in an infinite meadow, head down, constantly foraging and sniffing and munching. I stuffed words down urgently, as though the burning of the books was scheduled that day and, like the characters in Ray Bradbury's *Fahrenheit 451*, I had to embody each story for posterity.

It was and is love because I couldn't and can't live without them. Reading, like love, alters time. The state of having nothing to read is a dreary and intolerable reality. Once I was travelling through the mountains of Lesotho in southern Africa and our little convoy was marooned by torrential rain. We were stuck in a government rest house with very little to pass the time. I had just one book with me, Harper Lee's classic, *To Kill a Mockingbird*, but I had nearly finished it. The only other printed words in the place, and I can see them now, were the legend on a black-and-white poster of President William Tolbert of Liberia. The rain threatened to hold us there for days, and neither the book nor the poster was going to last long. I gazed out at the rain in despair. I was with people, but books can be better than people. Books are concentrated people, distilled life.

I must love books more than anything, because I would go mad without them and nearly did in that rainstorm in Lesotho. Books feed every part of me: my heart, my soul, my intellect, my imagination, my senses. I can't eat them, but actually, in a way that is what I do: eat, chew, savour, taste, digest books. And in return for my constant appetite, books give me the key to multiple worlds, from the universe itself, from imagined worlds like Troy and Camelot and Middle Earth, to the infinite world embodied in one other human character.

I might go blind one day, as my grandmother did, and then how would my love and I meet? We would meet as my grandmother and the world of books continued to meet in her blindness. In her nineties my grandmother taught herself to read Moon script, a form of raised lettering on thick paper. I have a photograph I took of her hand, with its veins and bones and freckled skin, feeling its way over the words and into another world. My grandmother loved books enough to teach herself a new way to read at an age when most people have stopped learning anything. Love makes you do things like that. If I have to, that is what I will do for the love of my life.

The Family Cuddle

Long before anyone invented the group hug, my parents and I invented the family cuddle. It was a lopsided one because when we stood in our small circle, our arms around one another, I was small and they were much bigger, so my head was somewhere around their waists. I got a faceful of sweater or apron, but that didn't matter. All that mattered was that I was surrounded by the arms, the feel, the smell of the people who loved me most, and I felt completely, utterly, indestructibly safe.

When I got older we went on holiday with another family, our friends and next-door neighbours, the Reason family, and I discovered the flip side of the family cuddle: the pain of exclusion from another group's closeness.

The Reasons had a car, which we didn't, and in those happy days before safety rules and seat belts, eight or nine of us would cram into it to go off for a picnic. I soon learned that the place to be was the back seat. The back seat was a loving place of giggles and closeness and sing-alongs and party mood and jokes. It was everyone huddled together and having fun. I was nine years old and I was sat sedately between the grown-ups in the front seat, while the other children enjoyed all this intimacy and carefree wonderfulness in the magic kingdom of the seat behind me. That's where love sat, and I wasn't sitting there.

I must have yearned and complained, because I remember that we stopped for our picnic and when we got back in the car everyone was allowed to sit differently. I was allowed to sit in the back. But wouldn't you know it, somehow that wasn't the place to be any more. The chemistry had changed and the party had moved on. Too many grown-ups had got themselves spread about, and that glorious feeling of the family cuddle on holiday had dissipated.

Years later I was on holiday with some friends and we all got cold and wet. Somehow I found myself exactly where I'd always wanted to be, crammed in and huddled right in the middle of the back seat with all the giggles and the hugs, and even though I was thirty years older it felt great.

My now-aged parents and I had a family cuddle again recently. It carried so much more emotional freight. They had both been ill, and I am sure we were thinking what we weren't saying, that we were all still here. And they were smaller with age. We had reversed. I was the strong one in the middle, holding these armfuls of frail people with their white hair. But we still giggled and held on to each other, overlaid by time on to the blueprint of those early cuddles when we were all young and healthy.

I have taken part in a few group hugs since then and, if the mood is right and you feel close to the people around you, they can be very nourishing. Love lies in many places, often waiting to surprise us, and sometimes it resists the forced growth of a hug between relative strangers. But when it works, I am happy to find it in those affectionate huddles where people who have been through something together, and care about each other, squish up close and the boundaries, for that warm moment, melt.

Meeting the Tribe

When I was a very small child love lay in the centre of my grand-parents' bed, right there where I could snuggle between their two warm, elderly, toothless bodies. My grandmother slept in a long flannelette night-dress. My grandfather was in striped pyjamas, and somehow he could make a transition between his night-time pyjamas and his daytime long johns without being naked in between. His teeth waited for him, pink and white and smiling, in a glass by the bed.

I could feel my grandparents on either side of me, radiating heat and love. They were laughing. I was burrowing further under the eiderdown, the blankets and the sheets to the safest place in the world, shielded from all harm and aggravation by two people who embodied affection and tolerance.

On top of my grandfather's head was one of the two special places in the world that I found on the bodies of those close to me. One was the gentle curve at my mother's waist, just where her apron tied, just above the soft shelf of her stomach, where I could rest my head as I stood, my arms around her, contentedly slotting in like a jigsaw piece. The other was the soft dent on my grandfather's bald skull, which caught the light and provided a perpetual target for my kisses, yielding beneath my mouth, my special place on my grandfather's head.

As the wider world comes into focus for a child there are special people waiting to pass on, quite unconsciously, their experience and interpretation of what the world is. You don't have to live in an African village or a Native American reservation to meet the tribe. If you did, things might be more clearly spelt out. There would be formal rituals for meeting and greeting you that everybody would know. As it is, it is only by looking backwards that I can see the ways of my grandparents and cousins and uncles and aunts for what they were.

As a little witness to the adult world, I was lovingly taught that grandfathers dug in their gardens and retreated to sheds. Grandmothers cooked in their kitchens and took me along to ritual gatherings with other elderly ladies in hats, who sat in circles and drank coffee and told me how much I had grown. Aunts were for picnics and presents and outings and being a bit naughty and subversive. Parents were for serious explorations of the world. They were for betterment and aspirations, museum visits and theatre tickets, walks in the country and explorations of the city. They tickled you and cuddled you, but they also made you do your homework and clean your teeth.

I didn't know, as a child, that all these people were simply human beings with weaknesses and ambitions and secrets of their own. It's taken my whole life to excavate their vulnerabilities. As a child I only ever saw their loving faces and lived in expectation of their gifts and treats. They taught me the dance of love. Love was given to me. I gave it back. My family, in all its manifestations, was always pleased to see me. I was pleased to see them back. Without ever saying the word, they were beginning my education in love.

Because they cared about me and I cared deeply about them, I learned, without being formally taught, to love other things than themselves. I adopted their love of certain foods and particular places. I imbibed their traditional pleasures and their educational values. I loved getting their approval, so I did the things they approved of, whether it was reciting the 12 times table, going to chapel or simply being charming to the neighbours. What is more powerful a social force than wanting to belong?

And, without mentioning the word "love", this tribe taught me to expect a love story of my own. Gossip was my education. I sat, silent, beside the behatted ladies, the little pitcher with big ears, and learned the fascination of liaisons and partings, broken hearts and happy meetings. Everything came to me in the form of a story, and my body responded to the emotional repertoire of shocked whispers, jubilant celebrations and conspiratorial laughter.

I knew, because everything and everyone around me was subtly preparing me, that one day it would be my turn. One day I would star in a drama. I learned that love had a hierarchy. Love for my doll or my books was real, love of my family was life-sustaining, but the life-changing love of my life would be between me and some boy, as yet unmet, who would be the One.

What they never told me, and what I never learned and had to teach myself, was that the One would never be enough. In adult life, when I had lived this central drama and come out the other side, I found that what I longed for most was this tribal love. I drew strength from the sustaining love that was embodied in all ages, both sexes and many different faces, and I tried to create it in other ways, through friends. And I consciously tried to create it for my children, because I know that the presence of, and the continued relationship with, an extended family are loving resources that last you all your life.

The Singer and the Song

Every child needs a tribe, and once I was privileged to see the tribe at work in someone else's world. My friend and I had missed the last public boat back from the beach in Turkey. The beach closed at sunset to allow the loggerhead turtles that nested there to come back from the sea and lay their eggs. The public boats had gone back to the nearby town, leaving a last few private boats and fishing boats tethered on the wooden jetties. If we were to return to the town at the far side of the river delta, we had to find a boatman who would take us before night fell.

In the thickening gold light of the evening an odd group was still sitting around a wooden table at the beach bar. One of them was the boat captain who the barman said might give us a ride. Next to him sat a grave-faced, dark-haired little girl about ten years old, in a pink frock, who seemed to be the captain's daughter. Next to her was a larger-than-life woman with a loud cigarette voice and a big laugh. She wore a dark dress cut low, had long dyed-blonde hair, and seemed to take up as much space at the table as the three young Turkish men who sat opposite her laughing and joining in scraps of songs with her. The little crowd of empty beer bottles and the laughing and the singing were clues that the party had been there for some time. My friend and I accepted a beer each and settled at the table, relieved that we'd found our lift home and also resigned to what could be a long wait.

The large blonde lady was singing a popular Turkish ballad in a deep resonant voice, and now and then the men joined in. Someone said that she sometimes sang in nightclubs. The little girl joined in once or twice. Behind her sat a traditional Turkish lady in headscarf and baggy trousers who laughed, but didn't join in at all. Another round of beer came. The pale stretch of beach turned a darker gold and the mountains grew a deeper blue against the evening sky. Then something unexpected and wonderful happened.

The little girl began, in a very quiet voice perhaps meant only for herself, to sing a song, and the raucous lady heard the little voice rising from below. Smiling, she stretched out an embracing left arm and placed it around the little girl's shoulders. With her right hand, palm uplifted, she gestured and coaxed the little seedling song out into the world.

The three young men, catching the tune and knowing it, began to join in loudly and drowned the little girl's small soprano with their cheery, beery bellow. The older woman silenced them with an imperious outstretched hand, like a traffic policeman. "Stop!" her hand said, then she turned in and down to the little girl and, with the most tender and loving encouragement, began to grow the song back out of her.

The group fell respectfully silent. The waves crunched and crisped on the sand and the little girl sang, at first very quietly, then more loudly. And as she sang the older woman created a loving space around her, which opened as the little girl's voice grew stronger and braver. In the circle of that woman's protection and attention, the child and her song bloomed with a spellbinding power that held us all still and entranced. When she finished we all cheered, and the little girl laughed and blushed with pleasure.

Later we did get on to the boat, and the captain let the little girl in her pink dress take the wheel and pilot us all through the twisting channels of the delta reed beds towards the town quay. The child had a look of perfect contentment on her face as she captained the ship back home. I felt I was looking at a child who had been given the rare chance to express herself fully in the magic circle provided by love.

When the Love in Your Life Isn't Human

When I was a little girl I walked to school with another little girl called Joan. One morning I knocked on her door and a tear-stained, blotchy-faced Joan answered it, leaking misery. Her kitten had died. I didn't have a kitten and had never had a pet, and I didn't get it. "But it's only a kitten," I said heartlessly. "It's not like it's your mum or something."

I apologise to Joan, after all these years. I now know that you can let animals into your heart. I also know that for many people, animals are a much more satisfactory source of love and affection than unreliable, self-centred, confused human beings. When I had kittens of my own, many years later, I felt guilty about my infant callousness.

The love of animals is much simpler than the love of humans. Dogs are for those people who like to be depended on and told they are wonderful. I find the devoted attention of a dog a little demanding, so I am a cat lover. I love the instant feedback of a cat's purr, which tells you immediately that you are doing the right thing. I love the companionship of a cat, which comforts without possessing.

If you're really lucky the animal in your life might be something more exotic and interesting than a dog or a cat. I know people whose snakes wrap themselves around their waists, whose iguanas feel at home sitting on their heads. I realised I had let an animal become the love of my life when I was into horse-riding in my twenties. A man who was pursuing me at the time, with moderate success, said bitterly: "I thought we could spend the weekend together, but you're always off riding your bloody horse." I remember the horse too. He was black and velvety, sexier and more powerful than any man I knew.

Once upon a time in Ethiopia I had a dog, a cat and a duck. The dog, Boffy, made me feel guilty because I felt I should be training him better and giving him more attention than I did. It made me feel especially guilty when I realised that he knew exactly when my husband was on his way home long before I did. That was when I realised that the dog was far more attuned to us than we were to him.

The cat, Unimog, was wonderful company, except when he went off on three-day benders and returned, dark-eyed, ratty-furred and exhausted, to collapse on our bed and sleep. But he liked to sleep in my in-tray while I was working, and if I curled up with a book he would curve up against my stomach, his purr vibrating through me.

But the Aylesbury duck, George, was the best pet of all. He was head of the pecking order because a nip from his bill was very painful, and the dog and cat stayed out of his way. George was always busy. He was a constant source of entertainment as he pottered about the garden, waking us with his *sotto voce* quacking under the bedroom window as the sun rose, going insane with joy if we filled his swimming bowl with water.

We had to pass these animals on when we left the country, but once we had children we bought kittens of our own. I loved to see the way that a child out of sorts would find comfort and companionship in communing privately with their cat. The care and consideration of animals teaches children to be thoughtful and gentle and empathetic and, when the animals die, as they do, they give an early lesson in the transience of life.

The lives of our cats were not so transient. It was twenty years before the last one died, long after the husband and the children had left home. In that interim period in my own life, the cats – first two, then one – were the life in my house. They were waiting for me when I turned the key. They talked to me and I talked back. As soon as I settled in a chair or a bed they gathered by me, a purring heap of warmth. And they also made me feel guilty. I was a single woman now and my cats took the spontaneity out of my life. When the last one died I was sad but relieved too, because the care of an animal is a great curb on freedom and a serious responsibility. I didn't replace them.

What I miss is less the individual presence of each animal, and their physical warmth next to my body, than the presence of life in the house. An evening alone watching television is an evening alone. An evening alone with a cat or a dog for company is renewal and recharging. It soothes the mind, comforts the body and relaxes the heart.

For some people their animals are their *raison d'être*. For some people they replace human beings. I have yet to meet the animal I would rate higher than another human being, but I know that the presence of an animal can give great comfort and even a reason for living. If a very sad child told me now that her kitten had just died I would treat the loss seriously. I would know that something very big had happened.

Being Choosy

My friends, Penny and Catherine, and I went off to Brockham Bonfire together. It was a dark November night, Guy Fawkes' night, and all the villages round about had their bonfires and guys and fireworks. But Brockham was famously the best and biggest, and drew the most people and carried the biggest risk, or promise, of mayhem.

We were teenagers, and Penny and Catherine were on a longer rein than I was. They had been allowed to flirt with mayhem before. They were more worldly wise than me, more experienced, more confidently flirtatious, less naïve. It didn't take long before they disappeared and reappeared before me with what they had really gone to the bonfire party to find: a boy each and a look of contented triumph. "Why don't you try that one?" they said, pointing out another likely lad in the crowd. I must have pulled a face because they crowed, "You can't be choosy!"

They went off with their new boyfriends, and I went home alone because when they told me I couldn't be choosy everything inside me said, "Oh yes, I can!" I wasn't shocked that they'd picked up boys at a bonfire party. I was shocked that they were so undiscriminating and desperate. If you couldn't be choosy, what was the point? Was I supposed to settle for anything just to walk around with a boy on my arm? Was I supposed to settle for someone I didn't like the look of? Someone I didn't trust? I was sixteen years old, shy and inexperienced, and all of me thought my friends were talking rubbish. I still do.

I know all the dangers of being a perfectionist. I know the new statistics that show that the older and the more successful in life you are, the harder it is for you to find a mate. Not because people aren't out there but because, in a way, you have so much to lose. I know that your life can drift by while you hang on to a fantasy of Miss or Mr Right.

I also know that the people who do best in the love stakes are often truly friendly people, who are open and encouraging and give people a chance. These are also often the people who are most skilled at drawing the best out of others. And yet, they are also people who have a healthy sense of their own self-worth and their own boundaries. They may be friendly, but when it comes to pairing off they are certainly choosy or, to put it more kindly, discriminating.

I've never forgotten that night at the bonfire. I hope Penny and Catherine are happy. I am sure they learned to choose. I know that it is important to have non-negotiable qualities in the people you allow to enter your heart, and I don't mean large breasts or fast cars. I mean qualities like humour and kindness and intelligence and thoughtfulness and good temper. When I was younger I fell for a good head of hair and broad shoulders, and I also tended to fall for interesting, creative neurotics. I still get attracted by a good head of hair and broad shoulders, but I value kindness and perceptiveness and tolerance. My definition of interesting has changed, and I would run a mile from a neurotic. No matter how good looking they might be, I couldn't find anyone attractive if they were stupid or intolerant or arrogant or had a bad temper. So the answer is not to get less choosy. The answer is to choose better things.

A Day at the Fair

It was a spring day on the open hillside of Epsom Downs, the home of the famous Derby Race. I was fifteen years old, and I'd come to the races with a boy called Robin I fancied from school. We were wandering through the fair that always sprang up along the race course. The air was full of the smell of engine oil and chip fat and candy floss and crushed grass. The machinery that drove the rides, the waltzers and carousels ground noisily around us, the air throbbed with generators, and music blared above the sound of the engines. I could hear the sound of a harmonica and Bruce Channel singing "Hey! Baby", and at that moment, Robin took hold of my hand.

I was fifteen years old and I was walking hand in hand with a boy I liked. We moved through the fair. Everything danced around us to the sound of Bruce Channel and his harmonica. Waltzers waltzed. Swing boats swung. The horses of the carousel rose and surged. The air was full of colour and flashing light bulbs and motion and lightness. And because a boy had reached out to take my hand casually, without looking at me or saying anything, the day was full of possibility and poetry, and my heart danced and waltzed like a fairground ride.

I loved that and I still love it. I love the lightness of it, the sense of imminence. Love has so many dark aspects. It can be weighted so deeply with fear and insecurity, longing and jealousy. We move far too fast from those exquisite moments of possibility and delicacy. We rush to give our feelings form and expression and tie them down, but there the moment is in my memory, lighter than many moments, floating like a butterfly.

I never loved Robin. We were never more than friends. I don't even know what became of him, but there he is in my memory: a smile, a lovely light moment when his hand reached for mine among the fairground rides in the spring sunshine with Bruce Channel singing "Hey! Baby". Of course, I can never hear that song without reliving that moment. If we had fallen in love, become intense, I wonder if this little memory would have lasted. It might have been drowned out, like a butterfly caught in the tide And I would have lost this little postcard from the lighter edge of love, the one that makes me smile and feel fifteen again.

What I Learned from the French

When I was fifteen years old I was sent off to France to improve my French and I fell in love, which as everyone knows is the best possible method to practise and improve a foreign language.

I landed into a great feather bed of luck in those six summer weeks. I found myself in a delightful, embracing family who are still my friends. I found myself installed in their large beach-front apartment on the Mediterranean eating delicious food. And for the first time in my life, I found myself becoming part of a large group of sociable attractive teenagers, swimming and sunning on the beach all day and dancing under the stars and pine trees at night. For a quiet bookish only child from a Surrey village who'd never been out with a boy and never been part of a gang, it was almost as scary as it was fun.

I watched and learned. I bought a big sun hat and a string of beads in St Tropez. I slathered on the Ambre Solaire and got a deeper and deeper tan as I lay in the sun, and I peeped under my hat brim at the ritual politenesses on the beach each morning as everyone kissed and shook hands. I observed the coquetry, the whisperings, the longing looks that those golden boys shot at the lithe girls in their bikinis, and the laughter of the girls. I was far too timid to flirt, especially in an unfamiliar language, but I lay on my sun mat and watched and wondered which boy I liked most. Was it Pierre with the dimples and the long eyelashes, or Michou with his muscular shoulders and white teeth. Or was it those other boys who swung by astride their Mobylettes, nonchalantly barefoot and barechested in their jeans, cigarettes hanging sexily from the corner of their mouths?

There were impromptu parties at night and in the hot afternoons while parents retreated to have siestas, without adult knowledge, we played kissing games. There was a game of musical cushions, and when the music stopped you had to kiss the boy opposite. One boy slobbered and left your mouth all wet, and another boy ground his mouth on yours and made it sore, and another boy kissed in a way that was soft and searching and exciting. And those French teenagers would compare notes in a good-humoured, non-prurient, unashamedly technical way. They had a curiosity and a pragmatic frankness that was utterly new to me, a little shocking at first but refreshing and liberating. They talked about one another as sexual beings, and about their sexual experimentation, as openly and as often as they talked about food which, being French, was an awful lot.

Sex and food, I learned that summer, in my beginners' class, had a lot in common. Both offer huge prospects of pleasure. Both involve anticipation, experiment, tasting and tantalising, satisfaction of desire. It was acceptable to take a deep interest in food, to treat the choosing, the testing, the preparation of ingredients with as much importance as the finished meal. It was acceptable to taste many different dishes and compare them. And both sex and food were only enjoyed at their peak once the people involved had developed their tastes and technical skills with research and knowledge and practice.

I had my first real kiss that summer. A little group of us were walking back to the beach through the vineyards, and I was hand-in-hand with a boy I really fancied called Philippe. Philippe had blue eyes and longer hair than anyone else, and he wore a mohair sweater and faded blue jeans which frayed over his bare brown feet. As we walked under the tall railway viaduct Philippe turned to go home and he kissed me goodbye, a real grown-up French kiss with tongues. It went on for a long time.

What I remember was that the others stood patiently and watched in a friendly and unembarrassed way. When Philippe had gone, a golden brown-eyed blonde called Marie-Christine said cheerily, "Was that your first kiss?" and, "Does he kiss well?" What did I have to compare it with? He kissed well enough for me to want him to do it again as soon as possible. He kissed well enough for the ratio of thinking about, remembering, replaying the kiss to time actually spent kissing was about ten thousand to one.

A day later and the same group of us were in a back room of someone's apartment, all watching in the same cheerful spirit of inquiry while another couple – Serge and Liliane – obligingly demonstrated a way of kissing they called *La Sucette*, the Lollipop. And then we all tried it for ourselves.

So that was all. It was a summer of kisses and curiosity. There weren't even any persistently straying hands. But we were only fifteen. We were still learning, happy to be practising our technique.

And that's what I learned from the French: not just the self-confidence that comes from honing your own powers of seduction, but that love and its many behaviours aren't just things that get giggled about – or even experimented with behind the school bike shed. The French taught me that love is a life skill, and that kissing and flirting are social arts as well as private pleasures. Like the techniques of making a good omelette or choosing a good wine, they can always be refined and improved.

How Long does a Kiss Last?

When you're new at the kissing game, the question of duration is a piece of urgent technical information, rather like the problem of how to angle your head and where your nose goes. But the real answer to how long a kiss lasts is days, weeks, years.

A kiss is so pure an act of intimacy, so complete a symbol of entry and possession and exploration, that its impact can be shocking. The first kiss you share with somebody can be the moment when you know there's nothing there after all. It's just a snog. Or it could be take-off, the moment when you feel your feet are leaving the ground for a long-haul flight. It could take two years for this second kiss to end or it could take a lifetime. What gives a kiss this power? Why aren't I saying the same thing about the act of sex itself?

A kiss is powerful because it is the first point of entry. There may have been glances, words, touches, even hand-holding, but a kiss is the first overt piece of risk taking, the first real contact between the sensitive and vulnerable parts of ourselves, the first little piece of commitment. Up to the point of the kiss, everything else can have been chance. A kiss is the first bold move, the first deliberate response. It's the first chance of rejection.

Kisses come on a spectrum of feeling just as love does. I love all these kisses: the kiss you bury in a baby's neck or stomach, the kiss I used to plant on my grandfather's gleaming bald spot, the kisses my cat used to give me with his scraper tongue, the kisses of greeting I share with my friends, the kisses on the paper cheeks of the old or the plump edible cheeks of children. There are the kisses that ask questions: "Is it you? Do I have a chance? Shall we?" And the kisses that demand relief: "I want you. Now. Here."

But no kisses are more exciting or memorable than those early kisses. Giving answers: "Yes, I want you too." Making promises: "If you like this I could give you so much more." Demanding answers: "Do you like this? And this? And how about this?"

Those are the kisses that release powerful emotions. Those are the kisses that keep you awake at night. Those are the kisses that replay and replay, preparing the body to jump into love with all its ecstasy and risk of pain.

There are people who would rather skip the kissing, but that's to cut out all the subtlety, excitement, teasing, uncertainty and exploration. Years later it's not the hours in bed with a lover I remember. It's the explosion of certain kisses whose aftershock still ripples through me in waves of memory.

Virginity and How to Lose It

Before we lost ours, my friends and I spent hours talking about our virginity. We were obsessed with if and when to lose it, how and with whom. My friend Meg and I had hung on until we got to university, and we were under siege as never before. Our friend Rhiannon, on the other hand, was much more relaxed about the whole business, because she'd lost hers under a bush on Wimbledon Common after two vodka and limes. Meg and I were shocked at this, but there was an adult calm about Rhiannon. The dilemma was over for her. She knew, and we didn't, and every day presented us with the dilemma anew. The boys we were dealing with, like Rhiannon, were ahead of us on this.

We weren't of a generation that believed you had to hang on for marriage, but we were of a generation that had to deal with ineffective contraception, and nobody wanted to get pregnant. As I remember it, our thinking went something like this. We wanted to lose it with someone special. Once you'd lost it, it might be more difficult to say no in future because people would know you'd done it. And before you'd done it at all, the fact that you'd be losing your virginity made it a bit more of a big deal. Actually, I think that was the extent of our thinking.

My friend Penny had another kind of thinking. She decided that she just wanted to get the thing over with in a quite clinical way, and that she would choose someone who had some experience and to whom she was unlikely to become attached. Which she did, and I think it was quite satisfactory, although not nearly romantic enough for me. I didn't want it to be tactical and clinical. I wanted someone special. I had made a little internal rule for myself that if someone I fancied quoted Andrew Marvell's "To His Coy Mistress" – "Had we but world enough and time, this coyness, mistress, were no crime" – I would be theirs. But they never did, so neither did I. There may be a few middle-aged men who read these words and curse. Well, you had your chance.

When I did it, it was with Beatle. I was nearly nineteen and my heart had been set on Beatle for quite a while. He had floppy dark hair in a Beatle cut, which explained his nickname, and he had the smoothest, most satiny skin. He was feisty and funny and playful, and we both had eyelashes so long they were in danger of tangling when we kissed. Beatle was ready whenever I was, but he didn't push me, which I liked. It was me that decided I was finally going to do it, me that picked out my best sexy French underwear, me that told him I was staying the night with him.

So it was in a bed in a proper bedroom, and I was with a boy I loved and fancied and trusted and laughed with, and I was innocent and hopeful and calculating. Somehow it wasn't quite what I was expecting because, for all our hours of talk and all the reading and gossiping, I'd managed to stay surprisingly innocent. We never talked about sex at home when I was growing up, and sex lessons at my co-educational grammar school were delivered in an aura of pinkness and sweat by a horribly embarrassed biology teacher who communicated nothing but fear.

I'd met an erect penis before, but somehow I didn't realise they went in and out. I suppose I thought that somehow, once the boy was inside you, there would be one huge melting fusion, and you would lie there in perfect bliss until… What? I don't quite know. I'd never given any thought to the mechanics. So when Beatle heaved and thrust for a while and then said it was no good, he'd had too much to drink, I was perfectly accepting and not at all bothered. We did it properly a bit later.

And a day or two after that we were doing it again and this feeling began to build in me, an inner excitement, a growing intensity that mounted and blossomed into a glorious explosion of sensation that I'd never had before. "Oh," said Beatle, when I tried to explain it, "girls can come too." Well, nobody had told me. Was this possibly the best surprise in the world?

There followed a period of wanting it and doing it all the time, of lots of laughter and silliness and sexiness, and a glorious summer-long sense of liberation and elation. And in between, intense moods and jealousies and deception (him), and tearfulness and clinginess (me). Beatle went off to Paris with blonde Katie from the art college and lied to me about it. I don't even remember how we officially ended, but we were still friends and later even flatmates, and I fell in love with someone else and so did he.

A few years later I arrived at his door in the middle of the night because I was stranded, and we shared his bed for old times' sake. And then I didn't really see him again, not until a college reunion thirty years later, when we were both greyer and wider, but still with the same long eyelashes and still falling easily into the same teasing complicity. And I have never, for one minute, regretted losing my virginity to someone who was sweet and funny and sexy and playful, as emotionally immature as I was but, as I enjoyed at the time and still know, many years and more experience later, a sensitive and considerate lover. It's worth hanging on for.

How to Have a Good Funeral

I was young when I learned how important it is to die well. When I was nineteen years old, my grandfather Bam, my father's father, died and I travelled north to Cleethorpes, the unfashionable, windswept seaside resort where my grandparents lived. It was in their house on a quiet avenue between the long sandy beach and the flat fields criss-crossed with little streams called becks that Bam had told me stories, oiled my first cricket bat, given me toffees, taken me fishing in the becks for sticklebacks, or let me potter with him and my gentle Great Uncle Walter, away from their powerful wives, in their old sheds on the nearby allotments.

I had never been to a funeral in my life. I thought I knew the people in my grandfather's life. This was my Northern tribe. I thought Bam mainly belonged to me, and my grandmother Nana, of course, and my father, and my aunt Mary and the other aunties and cousins. As we got into the car that drove us to the crematorium I suppose I thought, if I thought at all, that there would be this small handful of us saying goodbye. I had a physical sense of shock when I walked through the doors of the crematorium and found myself confronted with the backs of hundreds of people.

The room was full to the doors. As we were ushered to our seats I was bewildered. Who was everyone? Did Bam have a life beyond the garden, beyond the allotments and the becks, beyond the local cricket pitch and the bar at the Lifeboat Hotel?

I don't remember anything else about that funeral except that it was crowded with people I had never seen to whom my grandfather meant something. There were strangers who had loved him.

I remember my next funeral much more clearly, the one for my other grandfather, my mother's father, Grampa. I was in my twenties this time and I knew, through years of staying with my mother's family in the south Wales town where they lived and where I was born, that Grampa was a pillar of the community in an even bigger way than Bam. Each Sunday my Grampa took me to the Presbyterian chapel where he sometimes preached and was chairman of the presbyters. He had been a headmaster in the town, and had even survived the First World War and fought at Passchendaele, which is why he walked with a limp and a stick. I expected the crematorium to be full for him and, yet again, I was unprepared.

It is a Welsh tradition from my grandmother's generation that women don't attend funerals. We gathered at the house where my grandfather lay in his coffin, and the minister led us in prayer in the front room. My aunt stayed behind with my grandmother, while the rest of us went behind my grandfather in his hearse to the crematorium.

Of course the place was full, and this time I understood better who all these people were. They were the old men who had grown up alongside my grandfather, maybe even fought and survived with him. They were generations of men who had been taught and led by him as schoolboys. They were neighbours, fellow worshippers, men who felt my grandfather's passing as a real and personal loss.

They were mainly men, which is why, when they sang the hymns, their naturally harmonising voices vibrated the building with their power – an impromptu Welsh male-voice choir assembled for that moment by love and death.

I was so proud. I am crying as I write this, but I remember I felt both personal sadness and great elation. I could see it was a wonderful thing to be loved and valued by so many people. I understood, as my young soprano wove its silver thread into that heavy surge of bronze, that a good funeral is more than a righteous end to a life well lived, it provides a noble goal. It was a great gift to us, my grandfather's descendants, to witness the love and respect he generated. How could we not want to live life in such a way that we earned this kind of love and respect too?

I have been to other funerals since, and it is a privilege to be a witness to the passing of a well-loved and well-lived life. People leave these events uplifted, and I've often thought it a shame that the departed miss the best gathering of their life. It was this idea that made my cousin Susan invite the whole family to her mother's ninetieth birthday, because she knew we'd all meet at the funeral anyway and she thought it would be more fun if her mother was still alive. With impeccable timing, her mother – who loved a good party – died two days before the festivities, so we met at her funeral after all. And a good funeral it was, full of love and laughter, as the best ones are.

Weddings are not the only ritual for expressing and celebrating love. While the funeral of a young person is inexpressibly sad, the death of someone who lived their life to the full is marked by a solemn and loving rejoicing.

Safe Sex

There's no such thing as a condom for the heart. Until there is, there will be no such thing as safe sex. You can wrap your whole body up in protective sheaths, you can fill yourself with barrier creams and spermicides, you can have sex over phone lines and in cyberspace, you can have solitary sex all alone in your own brain, but the sex that leaves your heart and mind unscathed has not yet evolved. Until it does, what's safe?

We have AIDS to thank for the concept of safe sex. Before this deadly disease arrived in our lives, there was a brief flashing point in human history when, for the lucky few who had access to antibiotics and effective contraception (particularly the pill), sex became relatively trouble free. But only relatively.

In this brief historic period, sex required no forethought because a woman on the pill was always prepared. And men didn't have to think. There was no remembering to carry condoms or fumbling with them, thank the Lord. Nobody was afraid of sexually transmitted diseases, the ones like syphilis that used to maim and kill people, because we had antibiotics and we believed that everything could be cleared up with the right treatment. Even in this brief, relatively trouble-free interlude, things went wrong. Girls still got pregnant by mistake. People got crabs and herpes and worse. And the social pressure to have sex replaced the social pressure not to have sex, and led to its own unhappiness and error. If we had but known it, that was probably as near to safe sex as we were ever to come.

This lull didn't last long, as human history goes. As the threat of AIDS was realised and governments panicked, advertising campaigns urged people to put protective barriers between them to avoid deadly infection. Safe sex was the only sex. The free exchange of bodily fluids was over. The implicit promise of all this was that if everyone would practise safe sex the world would be a less dangerous place, but the only safety anyone thought about was physical.

There is no such thing as safe sex because sex is an elemental power. It can be benevolent or it can be destructive, and you often don't know in advance which way it will take you. It's not just that you might catch something, like a disease, or that you might become pregnant when you don't want to be, it's that everything changes when things become sexual, and the outcome of a sexual encounter is never predictable.

If sex were safe why would close friends hesitate to become lovers? It's because they know that sex changes everything, and that if they get it wrong they might lose a friend and then lose a lover too. If sex were safe why would sexual infidelity matter? Sex, in the context of infidelity, is highly dangerous, the cause of despair and heartache, even murder. If sex were safe why would whole families, even political parties, even whole societies, feel affected by an individual's choice of sexual partner? Because sexual liaisons affect dynasties and inheritances and politics and business. Sex isn't safe. Sex is a matter of life and death. Ask Romeo and Juliet. Ask Helen of Troy.

So there is no such thing as safe sex. There might be such a thing as effective contraception, although nothing is 100 per cent foolproof. There might be such a thing as effective sexual hygiene. But there is no kind of sex so safe that it will leave your body, heart and mind untouched. If it did, we wouldn't want it.

All sex with another person is risky, because the mind, body and emotions are one interconnected system. Germs may not cross a rubber barrier, but your mind can fantasise wildly, your heart will pound, your relationships will change and so will your understanding and concept of yourself. Nothing stays the same after sex. That is why it is so exciting, so intoxicating, so alluring. And why, even when it goes wrong, we keep coming back for more. They should tell them in schools, when they show them how to roll the condom on the banana, that this isn't the most important lesson in safe sex. What matters just as much in this high-risk human activity is how to protect the heart.

What is Love and How Do I Know When I've Fallen in It?

What used to be my nice well-ordered mind is seething with involuntary thoughts about someone else. This is one way I know I'm in love. I literally can't think about anything or anyone else. I am possessed. It's a kind of madness and it is exciting. People are impatient with me because wherever they are I am not there with them. My eyes are glazed and I forget what I am supposed to be doing. If I am alone, I spend hours in reverie. I replay his words and unravel his gestures, sucking out the last drops of sweetness from the sugar cane of memory. I recall his touch, and my body responds as if he were there in front of me. I have to keep doing this obsessive replaying because I need to reassure myself that it is real, this new person, this huge thrilling change in my monochrome life. That makes it sound as though I choose to do the replaying. I don't. It is the compulsive, out-of-control takeover of my normal mind that tells me I am in trouble.

It is so thrilling that my body is electrified. Even if the last fighting corner of my reason is struggling to keep order, my body, from the crown of my head to my toes, is out of my control. I blush, I flush, I quiver. I am uncoordinated and clumsy. My heart thuds and my insides lurch. I have lost all my dignity, although I try to appear cool. My exterior is as sophisticated and adult as I can make it, but inside I am fourteen again, no matter what my chronological age. My digestive system has gone on the blink, with the happy side effect that weight is falling off me, which means I can fit into new clothes, which means I feel more attractive. I find it difficult to get to sleep.

My reason tells me, through the turmoil, that I am in deep trouble here. Whether this is love or lust or infatuation, I am irrevocably in it and I won't climb out in a hurry. I need more than my rational mind. If I am going to be affected this badly, I need the strength of my wisdom, my spiritual connection, my intuition.

I need these forces with me because experience has taught me that symptoms this powerful and this irresistible are signalling a dangerous condition. This might not be the real thing after all. This might not be true love, but a fatal attraction that will bring me grief. The fact is that my heart and body are primitive and unthinking. They could be responding to physical and physiological triggers that won't be healthy for me in the long run. I could be blindly repeating a pattern that I need to avoid.

I need my wisdom and intelligence to slow me down. I need my powers of discrimination. If I am already in this emotional and physical state it is too late to escape unscathed, but I could still act wisely in the maelstrom. I could, for example, take a bit longer to get to know the real person who waits on the far side of my intoxicating fantasies. I could refrain from chucking in my job or risking my marriage. I could wait a little before I do anything irrevocable. I could find out if this person is good and kind as well as fantastic and fabulous. I could maybe get to see them in the context of their friends and family. I could behave as if I were my own wisest friend.

They don't call it falling in love for nothing. It is involuntary, mysterious and vertiginous. But falling isn't a sustainable state. Lasting happiness comes when you find your feet in love. You need to stand in love together, not lie winded in a heap. And that is what your mind is for, if you can hang on to it. It tells you which way is up. So when you've checked your symptoms and you know you're in love, remember that your mind is like your passport. Keep it in a safe place and don't set off on a long journey without it.

The More You Care,
the More It Hurts

Human beings are all so much frogspawn, a mass of tadpole cells joined together by jelly. A quiver in one corner sets the whole mass shivering, which is why I cry when television shows me a stranger falling out of a skyscraper in New York, or dying of starvation in Africa. But the nearer the next tadpole, the more powerfully you will quiver together, which is why the people I love the most in the world are also the people who upset me the most.

If I love someone, that means my emotional borders are open to them, and this is bad as well as good. Imagine you are walking down the street and you see a stranger across the road having a massive tantrum. The stranger is shouting abuse and acting in an aggressive way. You stop. You look. You think, "What's their problem?" And in half an hour you've probably forgotten all about it. A little emotional storm has gone off on a distant horizon and it hasn't touched you at all.

When I care for someone and am close to them, the dynamics are completely different. They don't have to explode. I can read the hidden tension in them on an emotional Richter scale. Their slightest mood shift goes through me like an electric current. In Cole Porter's words, I've got them "under my skin". Or, as the immortal P.G. Wodehouse put it, they are in amongst me.

My father can upset me so much that the tension I experience in his company when the emotional weather is dark affects me for hours, even days, despite my best efforts – and I know a lot of good ways of shifting tension. If my mother is ill and unhappy I can't rest or sleep for anxiety. I don't know how many hours, days, weeks I have spent in the obsessive reading of my lovers' moods, the better to understand and placate them. My children's moods affect me more than anything. I once measured my blood pressure after I'd had a loving conversation with my younger daughter, who is a calm person, and my blood pressure had risen which surprised me very much. I've since read that blood pressure always goes up if another person walks into the room. Human beings are not separate. We affect one another at the micro level.

If only love were a tension-free island, a refuge from the aggression and conflict going on outside its secure borders. That is how we like to see love, as a pair of welcoming arms. Imagine the familiar icons of love, the images that stand for emotional security: the lamplit circle of a family table surrounded by laughing faces, the mother cradling a sleeping child, the lovers' bed where two warm bodies lie smiling and purring in each other's arms in their nest of wrinkled sheets.

But the enemy is within. It walks in as soon as we open our heart and become vulnerable. What happens if the family is unhappy, if the mother abuses her child, if the lovers are unfaithful? Then the inner sanctum has been breached. Love's happy enclaves are less like rose-scented havens, more like the spaceship in *Alien* where the monster waits to burst out of our ribcage. They harbour the most shocking intruders of all, the ones who come in silently and take residence in your very heart.

How does this happen? It happens because the people who make you feel most invincible and invulnerable can undermine you most deeply. I don't mean that they hurt you on purpose (though they can). I mean that love opens the door to suffering in many ways. You hurt because you're joined, because there is no membrane between you, because you are part of the same organism. Children especially can break your heart. You would take a bullet for your child, but your unique punishment as a parent is to stand by and watch while the bullet hits them, and you can do nothing but mop up the blood and hold the wounded body. A child's sickness, failure, rejection and heartbreak are experienced by you with the extra twist of impotence and helplessness.

What I am saying is that pain is an inseparable and inescapable part of love. The deeper the love, the deeper the potential for pain. There is a global army of people who have sworn never to feel that bad again, even at the cost of putting the membrane back between their tenderness and the world. They look like everyone else, but something in them has decided to live apart – they are great people to fall in love with if you have a taste for unavailable lovers. Other people hurt and rise again. I admire people who are ready to take the risk again, but I believe in calculated risks. Some pain is unavoidable. Some pain you can see coming, even calculate. There are no medals for people who walk twice into the same fire.

Some pain is impossible to prevent, like the pain of knowing someone you love is suffering through illness, failure or heartbreak. Nothing can be done here but to stay alongside, offering what comfort you can. If you find yourself in this situation too often, taking on the habitual role of the sympathetic rescuer, take a step back. You may be unconsciously seeking out a situation that feeds a part of you better outgrown or abandoned. There is also little you can do after the event about the hurt that invades you when love ends, through parting, betrayal or death. Everything in life is transient, even undying love.

What you can do to minimise the part emotional pain plays in your life, without bricking up your heart, is to develop emotional antennae for the people and situations that could cause you trouble. Many people have an addiction to emotional turbulence and often create it where it doesn't exist. When you are young you can't be blamed for the emotional battering you might get, but you can be blamed if you helplessly seek out the same pain ten years later.

Somewhere between cauterising your feelings and being addicted to emotional turbulence lies a middle way. Cultivate self-knowledge, particularly of your emotional patterns. Know when your choices are self-destructive and seek help, if necessary, in changing them. And work on keeping your heart open, even at the cost of what Freud called ordinary unhappiness. There is no life without risk.

The Opposite of Love

If you ask someone what is the opposite of love, they invariably say "hate". I don't think hatred is the opposite of love, and the reason that I don't think this is because hatred is also a very intense emotion, which shares some of the core characteristics of love.

Like someone who loves, someone who hates is in thrall to the object of their hatred. Someone who hates is obsessed. Someone who hates worries at their hatred and often wants to express it physically. Someone who hates isn't free, because as long as you hate you are deeply bound to the thing you hate. What you hate is a defining influence in your life.

Some people think fear is the opposite of love and certainly, fear is also a strong emotion. Like love and hatred it has a gravitational pull. Unlike love and hatred the gravitational pull is inward, holding us small and leading us to run from and avoid what we fear. Someone who is ruled by fear is certainly in no position to love, because love demands courage. Love is the supreme risk, because to love is to lose control. To love is to open up and become vulnerable to pain and intense suffering.

If hate and fear are not the opposite of love, what is? I think that the opposite of love is separation. Love is what draws and binds people together. Separation is a free-floating hell. There are no forces of gravity at work here. The best on offer is indifference, a state of suspended animation that is not really living. At its worst, separation is a solitary confinement of the heart which makes us vulnerable to depression, loneliness and despair. It becomes a vicious circle of self-doubt and self-blame. This is why the sudden end of a loving relationship is so devastating. It throws us from the blessed state of union into the purgatory of isolation at a stroke. No wonder the experience can drive people mad, even make them kill themselves. The action of suicide is the ultimate expression of separation. It is a final cutting free from the overwhelming business of life.

In order to escape separation we don't have to rush indiscriminately into any sort of relationship. When these needy relationships go wrong, as they must, the feelings of separation are intensified by a sense of hopelessness. It helps to think small, on the scale of one action at a time, one day at a time. It helps to imitate the actions of love.

If I feel really broke I make myself give money away. Love is active. Love shares. Love is benevolent. Love is sociable. In order to imitate love, a person in a state of separation has to take action and initiate contact with other people, no matter how small the gesture. That could mean walking down the road to have a chat with the local shopkeeper, or it could mean throwing a party. Throwing a party is probably many steps too far for someone who is sunk in a separated state. For people who have drifted so far from the herd that they see no way back there are the Samaritans. There is always someone there to listen, even if it is to the silence of someone who has run out of things to say.

There are many small, manageable steps to joining the world. I know that people are mostly grateful to the person who makes the first move. Too many friendships go cold because one side thinks it is the other side's turn to make the move. If money for a drink or an outing is a problem, friends are often happy to meet for a walk. Almost everyone likes to go to a movie. If the idea of seeking out company for an outing is too great, go to a movie on your own and alter your thoughts and feelings that way. Anywhere is better than the inside of your own head in a separated state.

Everyone is grateful for offers of help, and helping other people always makes the helper feel better. If you have felt like trying out the new gym or renting a bike, it's likely that someone you know has thought of it too and would like to go with you. The many people who are worse off than you are waiting for help with their shopping or reading or to be given a lift. The way out of separation starts with a short walk or a phone call, and if that reaching out is to offer your services then you are no longer separate. You may not have found love, but you have become a source of loving kindness for someone else.

The Hunting Masks of Love

Once upon a time I made a mask of my own face in a workshop, and I coloured it blue, green and silver. I made my mask into the likeness of a moon-maiden, since that was my mood at the time. The mask was me and yet it wasn't me. It was directly modelled on my own physical features, laid on strip by plaster strip and hardened into a shell to be lifted off my own face in one clean pull. If you have ever made masks you know that this peeling away of the mould is an eerie moment. Where there was one face in the room now there are two: one living, breathing, human face reborn from the dead white plaster; the other a simulacrum of life, still and unbreathing, but radiating a lifelike presence.

Someone I loved at the time came to my house and became transfixed by my painted mask, hanging on the wall. He stood before it and he paid my plaster face an attention that my real one hadn't received in a long time. He even reached out his hand and caressed the plaster lines and contours while I watched him, happily enraptured to see someone so beguiled by an aspect of me.

"Don't get me wrong," he said, "I mean, you're beautiful. But this mask is even more beautiful."

Well, of course it was. It was a mask. It was clean, pure, smooth, unblemished. It had no worry lines, no angry frowns, no scars or spots, no uncomfortable gaze. It was the flawless beautiful version of myself, the face I would love to present to potential lovers if I could only sustain it.

Here's a huge irony about love. We want someone to fall for our true self, but we only go hunting for love behind masks. What we all long for, deep down at our most vulnerable core, is the miracle of someone who will love us no matter what. We want to be loved when we are stupid and mean, vain and short-tempered, selfish and thoughtless. We want to find the One who will love us so deeply that they will forgive us our withdrawn moods, see right past our big nose or blemished skin to the lovable us beneath. Yes, even those many people who think, "If you knew what I was *really* like you wouldn't love me."

And how do we go about this? By going out into the world behind layer after layer of masks. The people who know us best, our friends, our family, know us in all our complexity. They know us in our unwashed, unmade-up, grunting, farting natural state. But nobody goes on the pull in a natural state. We seize the props of make-up, hair products, discarded clothes edited out and dropped on the bedroom floor, the repertoire of expressions borrowed from film stars and practised in the mirror, the chat-up lines, the courage-boosting shot of alcohol, the posed cigarette, the dance-floor moves.

I know what my mask is and it doesn't work any more. It is a mask of indifference. I learned to put it on very early in life to stand between me and trouble. Nobody was going to get the satisfaction of seeing that they had upset me, because that would be to lose face. I was so successful at hiding my feelings that people assumed I didn't care, and that aggravated them. My headmistress gave me a dressing-down once because of my lazy don't-care ways, and she told my mother afterwards that the only way she knew she was getting through to me was a pulse that was beating madly in my throat.

It's only as I have grown older that I wonder how much this cool appearance has cost me. Maybe there were plenty of times when I would have liked people to persist, to penetrate behind this mask and know what I was feeling. But it was so well in place that they passed me by, not knowing that I was interested or that I cared. It's safe behind a mask of cool, but lonely too.

The fact is that masks have a limited use. They are so one dimensional. Are they really doing the work you want them to do? There's the life-and-soul-of-the-party mask, the everything-you-say-is-absolutely-fascinating mask, the you-don't-impress-me-much mask, the I've-got-everything-absolutely-sussed mask. They will all let their owners down one day. The masks get you through the door, but they won't keep you where you want to be. And all mask-wearers have those moments of wondering why someone they were interested in wasn't clever enough, didn't care enough, to see the real person behind the persona.

I like the lady who went off to meet the Queen and was asked if she'd put on her best manners. "I only have one set of manners," she said. I like the special people who are their natural selves with everyone they meet. They are neither cool nor gushing. They are confident enough in themselves to be genuinely interested in other people. They can be friendly without being misunderstood. They don't play games, and what a relief that is.

Dropping the mask doesn't mean facing the world unshaven or unmade-up. It doesn't mean being blunt to the point of rudeness. It is brave behaviour, because if you meet rejection it's you that is being rejected, not the part you chose to play that day. But the relief of meeting someone who is content to be themself is that you can drop your own mask at once. Being your unmasked self is the best and quickest way to meet the reality in other people. And it is what we all want, because the quality that defines the special people in our lives is that, with them, we can relax and be our own true self.

Fifty Ways to Leave Your Lover

It is always better to be kind. It is always better to protect some-one's ego if they have done you no harm, and sometimes even if they have. It is cowardly to run away. It is cruel to cut off communication. Nevertheless I ask forgiveness, because I have done all of the following unkind things.

I have said I would meet somebody and just not turned up; said I would ring them back and not rung them back; rung up and said I've found somebody else. I have written the letter that says I've found some-body else; left home rather than be there when they arrived; lied that I was leaving home in order to stop them arriving in the first place. I have set eyes on my summer love after a winter of writing love letters and realised instantly that this summer I wanted a new love; sent casual replies to men who had written that they loved me; eaten dinners that men had bought or even cooked for me and then made my excuses and run; sat in cars and taxis and said thank you for a lovely evening but I am not going to ask you up, goodbye. I have handed out a false phone number to somebody I was too cowardly to tell not to call; walked silently on a beach with a puzzled lover I shouldn't have gone away with in the first place; laughed at a man who was making a serious offer; frozen people out instead of having the courage to say what I really felt.

In my turn, and to serve me right, I have had all the following things done to me. I have watched more than one man walk out of the door even though I begged him not to go; lain awake all night more than once in an empty bed, counting the hours in solitary and growing disbelief, as the man who was supposed to come home didn't; waited at the station for the man who was letting me know by his absence that we were through; received postcards from Paris posted for a boyfriend by his friend, when the boyfriend in question had actually gone somewhere different with another girl and lied about it; cooked our regular lunch for the boyfriend who decided he'd had enough and just didn't turn up or call, ever.

Sometimes I managed the end with grace. Sometimes people ended gracefully with me. Sometimes people accepted my departure with a grace that made me cry, like the man who wrote a beautiful letter to say that many places, indeed one whole city, Paris, would never be the same without me. Now that was stylish. Ending is always hard, but he taught me that even in defeat you can end up on the moral high ground. But then he was older than me. Skills like these, and the empathy that reinforces them, take a lifetime to learn.

Narcissus and the Art of Self-worth

I hear people say it all the time: "You can't love anyone till you love yourself." I hear it and I groan. Loving yourself, how self-centred and narcissistic is that? Most people in the culture I grew up in – post-war, puritanical, stiff upper lip and pulled together – would react the same way. But the culture has changed. People don't pull themselves together and brace themselves anymore. They pamper themselves instead. Books, workshops and magazine articles all bang on about the importance of loving yourself, but what does loving yourself mean? Don't you have to know yourself first?

Narcissus loved himself and it got him nowhere. He was a beautiful youth who gazed at his own reflection in a pool and was so transfixed by his own wonderfulness that he fell in self-love and became rooted to the spot. The beautiful boy became a flower, condemned to be stuck in a vase for eternity. Self-love, in this myth, is a self-regarding, circular, ungenerous thing. Why would this be good? Aren't we in danger of becoming a generation of narcissists? Babies are narcissists, drawing in love from every source and developmentally incapable of the acts of reaching out, self-restraint and empathy that recognise that they are not the centre of the world. Adult narcissists are a pain in the neck.

And yet there must be another kind of self-love. Jesus Christ said that we should love our neighbour as ourself. If he didn't mean we were to love ourselves somehow, this moral command would have no meaning. Every religion has this central message, that the secret of goodness and of love in the world is to do unto others as we would have them do unto us. It follows that if we feel worthy of kindness, generosity, goodness, thoughtfulness, care and consideration, then we should automatically offer these in our dealings with other people. A sense of self-worth, but not self-importance, gives people the openness and confidence to build loving and giving relationships.

If you want to know how people behave in love when they don't love themselves or, as I feel happier thinking of it, when they have no sense of self-worth, look around. They make other people supremely uncomfortable, even miserable. When you lack self-confidence you feel insecure, jealous, needy, over-demanding and manipulative. Instead of giving love in a fair and free exchange you find ways to steal and grab it, and you always fear that it won't be returned.

When you lack self-worth you try to drag other people down with you by destroying their confidence. When you lack self-worth you will put up with abuse and maltreatment because, deep down, you agree that's what you deserve. You think that this is the way love comes, and you are more afraid of losing the bad deal you have than of the even more worthless feeling of being alone. People who have a strong sense of self-worth enjoy their own company. They grieve for lost love, but they don't assume that they deserve unhappiness.

I've done my share of manipulation and needy whining in my time, and you may get a short-term return but it's not healthy in the long term. You can pressure someone into saying they love you, but they feel manipulated and you are unsatisfied because the gift was forced and therefore worthless.

I've noticed that people who have a strong sense of their own value are not interested in power games or neurotic moodiness. They don't want to waste time in relationships walking on eggshells or placating bad temper. They would never attract a partner who hit or abused them because their antennae are tuned to respect and equal treatment.

It is hard for people who have not received the right amount of love in babyhood and childhood to feel a sense of self-worth, but you can re-parent yourself in adulthood. Happily, there are plenty of ways to build the sense of self-worth that makes life worth living. Above all, self-worth is built by doing. Self-worth comes with learning a skill, playing a sport, taking up running, learning to dance, sing, play an instrument, learning another language, volunteering, taking on responsibility, organising an event, raising money, getting involved in your community, building expertise in an art or a craft, going on a difficult journey. Not only will you feel a whole lot better about yourself through the act of doing and joining in, but you will meet more interesting and worthwhile people and enjoy life a great deal more.

Self-worth and self-enjoyment come with activity not passivity. Of course this reflects itself in the way you relate to other people, and it hugely widens the circle of people you can relate to. Beware the self-love that separates you from life, like Narcissus by his lonely pool. What's the point in knowing you are wonderful if you can't find anyone to agree with you?

Fatal Loyalty

Love is the most urgent call to self-knowledge. It is in our relationships with other people that we learn our shortcomings or test our powers of giving and unselfishness. Sooner or later, in many people's lives, these lessons become so urgent and so painful that people turn beyond the relationship and beyond their own social circle for guidance. It doesn't matter how cool or how experienced a person is. Secretly or overtly, they are always curious to know how this thing works.

It begins, in childhood, with the agony aunts. I remember the magazines with their problem pages hidden under the desk in the school library, telling us about problems we hardly knew existed. Now there are special problem pages for teenagers read by pre-teens, which talk about "lurve" and give information on contraception and blow jobs.

The more practice you get, the more urgent is the need to accumulate knowledge and understanding as your mistakes get bigger and graver. Millions of people, over decades, have gone to marriage guidance or relationship counselling. Many of them learn what I learned, in a brief session of marriage guidance, which is how little we really listen to each other and how painful it can be when we really do. But if you want to learn even more about the workings of love in a relationship, then you need to know about far more than just what happens between the two of you. You need to become archaeological.

I have done two processes in later adult life that I wish I had done sooner. Both taught me profound lessons about the root sources of our ability to love, and how we can reclaim and reshape them. Both deeply affected my view of my family and my intimate relationships.

The first process is called the Orders of Love. It was originally developed by a German priest-turned-psychotherapist called Bert Hellinger, and it is now taught internationally. Its underlying thesis – developed over many years and synthesising what he learned through working with the Zulu peoples of South Africa, and with further work in Western psychotherapies – is that love flows naturally through families and down the generations unless something happens to block it. Where there is an emotional problem in an individual, its cause is often a trauma or blockage further back in the family, which has distorted the flow of love. An Orders of Love workshop is an extraordinary and, to me, deeply mysterious and moving process, which involves participants nominating others to act out the roles of their family members and then watching as the unconscious drama unfolds. These groups of family members are called constellations. By physically positioning these people instinctively in relation to one another some alchemy happens, in which participants involuntarily express the emotions felt by the original family members, even though they know nothing about them. With the skill of the facilitator, who moves people about and brings others in, the original family trauma is uncovered. And then the facilitator creates a ritual of acknowledgement and forgiveness, which liberates the original participant from their family role of unconscious duty and loyalty.

The noble aim of this work is to break the invisible but sometimes fatal loyalties that bind families together, even in unhappiness, and break the chain for future generations. I have twice spent the weekend doing an Orders of Love workshop and been profoundly moved by the process. Taking part in other people's constellations feels like a great privilege.

There are connections between the work done by Bert Hellinger and his followers and the work done in the Hoffman Quadrinity Process, which is also taught internationally. Bob Hoffman's genius was to synthesise a number of forms of psychotherapy into an intensive eight-day residential process, which goes deeply into the way in which participants have learned about love through their families, and enables them to release the bad and deeply acknowledge the good. Both Hellinger and Hoffman acknowledge the intense and invisible power of what Hoffman calls "negative love", that unconscious and self-limiting loyalty towards our families which leads us to adopt family roles and to suppress and sacrifice ourselves on behalf of family values, even when these are destructive. Hoffman also saw the human personality as being fourfold – an emotional, intellectual, physical and spiritual self – and the work focuses on giving each of these aspects of the self a voice, and integrating these aspects through the course of the week.

The Hoffman Process is longer, more intensive, more explicit, more structured and better designed to integrate into your life than the Orders of Love. It leaves you feeling exhilarated but also grounded, with a bag full of techniques you can use once you leave the workshop environment. It also provides you with valuable backup from the Hoffman community, and a network of participants who can help reinforce what you have learned. The experience of Orders of Love is less integrated into normal life though it works well with therapy, but it is also profound, especially when you take part in other people's constellations and have the extraordinarily mysterious feeling of embodying the emotions of strangers. Each time I have done an Orders of Love workshop it has made me deeply question the separate nature of the individual human personality. On the contrary, it has shown me clearly that we aren't separate at all. We are simply cells in one infinite human body, past and present, and, in the right circumstances, the experience of one is the experience of everyone. The boundaries between us are infinitely fine. This may be the message of the mystics, but in these two processes you can experience it.

Why would you want to give up your time and money to do this kind of work? I know that many people I meet, especially those who are disinclined to examine their emotions at the best of times, would rather break a leg than do what they would call "wallowing" in emotion with strangers.

Well, why wouldn't you? Love is the central mystery and the greatest challenge of our lives. I read the story of a man who had nearly lost his life rowing across the Atlantic. He asked himself why he was prepared to face death on the open ocean but found his personal life so difficult. "I think what it is is this," he wrote. "When you are involved with other people, lovers and loved ones, it's not in your control." Somehow he found the challenge of the Atlantic simpler than the challenge of other people.

I can understand this. When I get it wrong in love the results can be devastating, for me and for other people. What I've learned through the work of Bert Hellinger and Bob Hoffman is that we *are* other people, and that knowledge is transformative. I have cried and laughed through these two processes, felt intensely, thought deeply. They have brought me some understanding and compassion, helped me open doors and mend fences in my own life, and given me insight into the roots of my own and other people's behaviour.

Love isn't a theory, it's an experience and, above all, a practice. In carefully evolved processes like these two, conducted by trained and responsible people, you learn about love through direct experience, and it can change the way in which you lead your life. What I also like about these two processes is that the people who run them aren't evangelical or pressurising in any way. They only want people who really want to be there, doing the work when they are ready to do it. I wish I had found them earlier in my life. The details of how to contact these two organisations are at the back of the book.

Everyone Has Baggage

When you've been around a bit and you're looking for love again there's a phrase you'll often hear people using. "She's OK," they'll say, "but there's a bit too much baggage for me." What they actually mean is that there's a long emotional CV. There are outgrown relationships, maybe even a marriage or two and, worse, there may be children. There you all are at the starting tape for the next race, and the person with all those encumbrances is handicapped before they begin.

The people who hold out for partners without baggage want somebody with an unsullied uncynical heart, and they don't like competition, not even from their new lover's children. Some long for an unsullied virginal body as well, which narrows the field even more. They don't want any nasty surprises on the road ahead, no lovers leaping out of the undergrowth offering their kiss-and-tell stories to the highest bidder, no children turning up on the doorstep, suitcases in hand. They don't want a lover who has lived a life, although, in my experience, they don't apply the same rules to themselves.

The truth is that everyone has baggage. The human being who is a pure *tabula rasa* doesn't exist. The most famous and least successful case of looking for baggage-free love was the marriage of Prince Charles and Princess Diana. Diana was supposed to be young, virginal, innocent and easily moulded. Well, we all know how that worked out. She ticked all the boxes, but she came with baggage nonetheless. She had a childhood badly affected by the divorce of her parents, and an idealistic dream of fairy-tale love that was shattered before the wedding day. Charles had plenty of emotional baggage of his own, including a married woman he would rather have married himself and eventually did. The result was the slow public disintegration of a so-called fairy-tale marriage.

I repeat: everyone has baggage. In societies less wedded to individualistic romantic love matches than the affluent West, the family is every bit as important as the bride and groom. It doesn't matter what culture you live in, you really are marrying your mother-in-law and her sisters and her cousins and her aunts, so it is wise to open your eyes and take in the whole picture. Pay special attention to your beloved's relationship with his or her parents, and to the parents' relationship with each other. Sooner or later you may find yourself being turned into your own mother- or father-in-law and replaying the past despite yourself. Forewarned is forearmed.

There are other, less visible kinds of baggage. There is your lover's unspoken desire to change you, the unshared ambition to live a certain way, the desire to have or not to have children, the genetic tendency to grow fat and lazy or drop dead of a heart attack, a filthy temper that is hidden in courtship, a tendency to depression that is hidden by the euphoria of love. How many people have you heard say, "It was all going so well and then he completely changed character." People don't really change character. It's just that their baggage was delayed on the way but it has finally arrived.

Unexpected baggage is yet another reason why the greatest emotional challenge for human beings is to sustain a loving relationship with another human being. You don't always get what you think you're getting, and then it is too late. This is why the successful relationship has to be like an expanding suitcase, a thing of infinite capacity.

Do You Still Have Paris?

Most of us get to conduct our love lives in offices and back streets and housing estates and bars and parked cars and in front of the television. It's worth saving for a ticket to a better backdrop because a great location gives love a lift. Even if the affair ends, the hand you held strolling along the Seine or sitting by the Taj Mahal will stay in your memory forever. Like Bogart and Bergman in *Casablanca*, whatever happens to you, you will always have Paris.

When I look back at my life it's the times I spent in exotic locations that stay with me, while the years of life I have passed in my normal habitat of London and England simply run into a blur. That's why I'm a great believer in the holiday romance. Of course it's easier to feel romantic on holiday in a beautiful unfamiliar setting, often with someone you may not see again but will never forget. When you travel, your senses are heightened, your antennae alert. The whole experience of a new place and a new culture is magnified when you are seeing it hand-in-hand with a new love, and that city, that view, will always have a place in your heart because you saw it through a benevolent haze of hormones.

Thanks to love I have romantic memories of France, Greece, Japan, Israel, Tanzania, Ethiopia, Italy – places where the thrill of discovering another person was expanded by the setting of an Indian Ocean beach or a tropical rainforest, a Greek ferry or a Parisian restaurant. There is a downside to this. If you can only find love away from home, you may be a person who has a pattern of loves that don't last. Male or female, too much love on the run is the sign of someone who is afraid of commitment. And, if you only get to experience love on holiday, then it might be worth looking more closely at the way you live your life at home. In particular, I am not recommending sex tourism, the kind where, male or female, you travel abroad to find sexual satisfaction with somebody poorer and less powerful than you are.

I'm talking about love between equals, and the boost that landscape can give to a love that lasts. I met my Scottish husband on a Greek island. We spent an idyllic week together walking thyme-scented rocky hillsides to the sound of cuckoos. We married in Ethiopia and went to live in Afghanistan. We separated years ago, but those early years still bond us. We still have Addis Ababa and Masawa, Lake Haik and Lalibela, Kabul and the Minaret of Jam.

I married the man but I didn't want to spend my life in the exotic landscapes, which is one reason among many that the marriage didn't last. There's only so much sustenance you can get out of a beautiful view. Some people fall for the view too, and end up married to a Masai tribesman or a Greek fisherman. Sometimes this works out, and sometimes it doesn't, in which case it's less a case of having Paris, more a case of Paris having them. But, however the story of their love ends, it is richer and more interesting than it would have been if they'd just stayed at home.

My Wedding Day

I like a love that tells a story, and everyone knows that the wedding day is the happy ending of the story of one's single life. It is also a story complete in itself, with a beginning, a middle and an end. It has costumes, lights, supporting cast, music, subplots. It is so thrilling and significant a drama that many people, certainly most women, dream about their wedding day from childhood, imagining the sets and props before they can visualise the face of the person who will be standing next to them. No matter how much I dreamed, I could never have come up with the way my wedding actually was. This is the true story.

The story began when I met my future husband on the Greek island of Rhodes. He was a young Scottish doctor escaping from long hours on a busy paediatric ward by catching a last-minute, very cheap holiday flight. I was a young journalist on holiday with my friend Valerie, staying in a shared villa in the picturesque little town of Lindos. We were partying on a villa rooftop one night when Valerie came out of the crowd leading a young man who was wearing a floppy black felt hat and a straggly Viva Zapata moustache. "L," she said, because that's what she called me, "L, this is Dr Ken."

Over the next week Dr Ken and I got very drunk together, escaped to another island, walked on springtime Greek hillsides breathing in the scent of wild thyme and listening to the cuckoos. He told me about the mountains he'd climbed, and we talked about the adventures we wanted to have in our lives and how we'd love to give up our jobs and go travelling. On the beaches, among the rocks, by the sea, we wondered why life couldn't always be like this. He had to go back to London earlier than I did, and by the time I arrived home I was astonished to find that Dr Ken was as good as his holiday word. He had resigned his job and was already applying for overseas postings. I was so inspired by this resolution and vision that within a month I had left my newspaper job. My future and Dr Ken's were already linked.

Within the year we were living together in a tin-roofed, pink-and-green-washed mud-and-straw house over 8,000 feet up the mountains in the Highlands of Ethiopia, with a dog, a cat and a white Aylesbury duck called George. My Scottish boyfriend had taken a job with Save the Children, setting up rural health programmes in the northern provinces of Ethiopia. Sometimes I travelled with him through the astonishing mountain scenery, sometimes I stayed in our little house with the dog and the cat and the duck, and tried to carry on my writing career. As the months went by we decided to get married.

There is a shortage of wee kirks among the heather in Ethiopia. We thought it would be very romantic to take the old steam train from Addis Ababa to the former French colony of Djibouti on the Red Sea coast, and get married there with the bonus of French food and champagne. Then a skirmishing war broke out between the Ethiopian government and the Afar tribes in the desert to the east, and the train stopped going through to Djibouti, so that was out.

So we thought it would be very romantic to get married at the British Embassy in Addis Ababa, but the British Embassy told us that where there were perfectly good marriage laws, its citizens overseas had to get married by the law of the country they were in. So we published our banns in the British Consulate and booked a date in the Registry for Marriages, Divorce and Death in the giant modern concrete fortress of the Addis Ababa Municipality.

I fell into some gloom about this. I hadn't been much of a fantasist about my wedding day, but it didn't include office blocks and no poetic vows. I wanted some poetry, some public declaration, some ritual, the comfort of the familiar words of a marriage ceremony, even a civil one. But my future husband told me to pull myself together, and that I sounded as though I was more interested in the form of the wedding than the more important fact that I was marrying him. So I shut up and took comfort in the business of finding a wedding dress.

The Ethiopian national dress for both men and women includes a fine cotton shawl called a *shamma*, which comes in pure white with many variations of embroidered border. Ethiopian women wear it over a white-cotton waisted dress with a gathered skirt, which looks like a child's first communion dress. I toyed with the idea of marrying in a white *shamma* but, truthfully, it was a bad idea and I looked awful in one. Fortunately, Addis Ababa had one smart Western-style boutique, run by a former Air France stewardess, and it was there that I found a simple pale-peach-coloured dress that felt sufficiently bridelike to do the job.

On the morning of the wedding the bride and groom sat up in bed together in the Ghion Hotel, Addis Ababa, and, since there didn't seem to be a moment for this in the official procedure, the groom put the wedding ring on the bride's finger. It was thrilling. The wedding ring had been made for us by a goldsmith in Dessie market and was a solid 14 grams of finest soft Ethiopian gold. When we got back to London I took it to a jeweller to be engraved inside with the words "Ken. Lesley. 30th Genbot 1968", because that was the date of our wedding (7 June 1975) on the Ethiopian calendar.

There was no family with us on that day, although there were telegrams waiting at Addis Ababa post office. Instead our friends arrived to take us to the registry office, and suddenly all my quivering shivering nerves vanished and I felt alert with conscious happiness. The morning in Addis was clear and sunny, with the clarity of the thin air that comes at 8,000 feet. The eucalyptus trees turned their blue leaves in the breeze. The streets, with their eroded edges and gullies, were crowded with normal Addis traffic: donkey trains trotting under loads of wood, shabby horse-drawn gharries taking shawled women to market, men walking barefoot in the habitual Ethiopian manner, their wooden staffs draped horizontally across their shoulders and their arms draped across the staffs in a human cross. Women and girls walked by bent under stacks of kindling or heavy clay water-jars. Dogs, children, chickens scurried under everyone's feet. The timeless living city hustled and bustled and we were on our way to get married and it was all so exciting.

The Princess Aurora had a bad fairy at her christening. I had a bigamist at mine. I don't blame this presence for the break-up of my marriage fifteen years later, but there was an ironic piquancy in the fact that one of our four witnesses, an English teacher working in Addis, lived with his British wife and children in one street, while he kept an Ethiopian common-law wife and children in a house half a mile away. He always said, as he rushed from supper with one wife to dinner with the other, that the trouble with bigamy was eating all the food.

The room in which we married, once we arrived at the concrete cliffs of the Municipality, was an anonymous concrete cell where we sat, Ken and I and our two witnesses each, side by side on torn leatherette banquettes, while the Ethiopian registrar slowly filled in a page in a very large book and passed it around for us to sign. Our reward was several marriage certificates, half in the higgledy-piggledy script of Amharic, half in English, all stapled with our photographs. And that was it. No words. No vows. No music. No public declaration of love and commitment. Just us, apparently Dr and Mrs Grant, rushing giggling out into the city, looking at each other like children, saying "We're married!" as though it couldn't really be true.

We ate lobster from the Red Sea and drank champagne at a table strewn with fresh rose petals in Castelli's, the best Italian restaurant in Addis Ababa. A huge romantic bouquet of pink roses arrived as a gift from the restaurant, and later in the afternoon we drank wine and ate wedding cake in our friends' garden. My favourite wedding photograph shows me with my arms full of roses and Ken with his arms full of George the duck, who belonged to our friends until we took him to live with us.

As the afternoon wore on everyone became more and more drunk, especially the groom. I am sure I'm not the only bride since the beginning of time who looked into a mirror on her wedding day and asked herself, "What have you done?" And with hindsight, my new husband may have been wondering the same thing, which might be one reason why he was so drunk.

At sunset our friends took us off to the railway station, where we climbed on to the overnight sleeper to Dire Dawa, down from the mountains and into the desert and a tropical climate. We woke to a flat hot landscape, where the women wore brilliantly coloured and patterned *shammas* and sold tropical fruit by the railside.

The next day my sober new husband and I sat at a shady table in one of Dire Dawa's leafy streets, and he was unusually quiet. "What are you thinking?" I said. "I'm thinking that now I'm married I'll have to get organised about things like life insurance," he said. It was the sweetest, most romantic thing he'd ever said to me. A year later, apropos of nothing, he said: "I sometimes wish I wasn't married, but then I'd meet you and fall in love and want to get married all over again." That was very nice too.

There's a Song in My Heart

You know it's love when prose simply won't do. When I was a teenager with a frequently bruised heart I sought refuge in poetry. I still have an old exercise book in which I copied out those poems that hit the spot. "Never give all the heart," wrote W.B. Yeats. Young, battered and cynical, I eagerly wrote the poem down. I was one with the disillusioned Yeats. "He that gives this knows all the cost, For he gave all his heart and lost." Me too, W.B., me too.

But somehow you keep giving your heart, and if you're lucky someone will give their heart to you and then your heart soars beyond the everyday. The language and rhythms of tax demands and newspapers are too plodding. You need music. You need rhythm. You need rhyme and metaphor. I know I'm happy when I catch myself singing out loud. I know I'm in love if I catch myself writing verse.

In the first year of my married life I exploded with songs. I remember the first days of our honeymoon in Ethiopia. I was lying on a sunbed in the enchanting gardens of the Galela Palace Hotel It overlooked a great lake, and the garden was full of trees which hummed and twittered with tropical birds. I must have started humming and twittering too, in my state of great contentment and happiness. I had never written a song in my life, although I had written poems. Over the next few weeks I was possessed by songs. They bubbled up from me and I sang them unaccompanied on to tape, those songs that reflected our life, happy together 8,000 feet up a mountain.

I sang about the way I felt waiting for my young husband to come home from his long field trips, about the cosiness of sheltering from the rainy season and the thunderous sound of the rain on our corrugated iron roof. I wrote songs about the games of poker we played with our friends and the candlelight we read by, and all of them were songs about being in love.

This is what happens when the heart is touched. It surges in a creative overflow. I see people in love making offerings of all kinds. Lovers find themselves doing uncharacteristic things, expressing themselves through poetry and paint, embroidery and knitting, flowers and food. The feeling that has taken us over is beyond sensible words and coherent phrases. With such a glorious confusion inside, only exuberant expression will do.

I miss them when they're gone, these creative fireworks. It does go, this welling up from a joyful source. The speaking-in-tongues phase of love rarely lasts unless you happen to be a poet, in which case it is your calling to go on expressing what everyone else feels. The rest of us calm down eventually and go back to speaking the impoverished language of the tabloid paper and the TV soap.

There is another impulse towards poetry and music. The end of the affair, if it comes shockingly, can have the same explosively creative effect, as we sob and rage our way on to the paper or the canvas. It can be hugely cathartic. And if you can't find the right words for how you feel then reach for the poetry books and the CDs, because Yeats and Shakespeare, Cole Porter and Leonard Cohen, Ted Hughes and Sylvia Plath have done it for you. And if you are not already listening to your favourite gloomy music, it is time you discovered that, whether you like your love as grand opera or sung to a lonely guitar, music and poetry are the release that makes the healing tears fall. As for me, somewhere I have an old home-made tape of songs from my heart that still tell me what it felt like to be a young bride, in Africa and in love.

Love and Peace

There is a growing practice, among those few people on the planet who have a great deal of money to lose, of entering into a prenuptial agreement. The many billions of us who do no such thing know about these agreements because we see them on the movies and read about them in the gossip columns. Prenups, as they are popularly known, seem controlling, pessimistic and untrusting to those of us who aren't film starts, but maybe it is sensible to divide up the spoils while the couple are full of warm feelings for each other. Dividing up the spoils in a spirit of resentment and bitterness only leads to more resentment and bitterness, huge legal fees and fewer spoils to divide.

The rest of us, who think we have no spoils worth dividing, are wrong. There are more things at stake than money. The accumulated emotional capital of a happy relationship is beyond valuation. It consists of happiness, contentment, support, security, productivity and deep peace of mind. It includes the greatest gifts of love, the gift of belonging and the gift of meaning. The loss of these when a relationship breaks up can be more painful than death itself.

Maybe there should be another kind of prenup. Not one that assumes defeat and divides the spoils ahead of time, but one in which both parties agree to face and resolve difficulties together in an agreed process which some call the Path to Peace. How I wish that I and my former loves had learned to listen to and negotiate with each other in this way. The precious emotional capital of a relationship is not usually lost in one cataclysmic coup, but squandered incrementally. An unhappy relationship rots from within over time, eaten away by the termites of anger, unkindness and mistrust. Signatories to a prenup of peace would have the means to shore up the relationship before it collapsed.

I first came across the Path to Peace in a workshop run by Seanna McGee and Maurice Taylor. It is discussed in depth in their book, *The New Couple*. I was struck by the simplicity of the process in practice – because it is relatively quick to do. In skilled hands it takes minutes. And I was struck by its subtlety, because it acknowledges and provides a means of expression for the layers of other feelings that lie beneath the surface anger. By disclosing the bad feelings honestly, and getting them truly heard by the other, it also allows the hurt person to see their own part in the dispute. And it ends with both sides feeling understood, open and ready to communicate again.

In its simplest form, the partner who has a grievance to air suggests the Path to Peace and the other agrees.

In Step One, the speaker explains what has made them angry, and the other repeats their words back to them. For example, the speaker has been left waiting on the street because the other was late.

In Step Two, the speaker expresses the hurt and sadness that lie under the anger, and the other repeats their words back to them. For example, the speaker is upset that he was kept waiting because this made him feel unimportant and uncared for.

In Step Three, the speaker expresses the fear that underlies the anger and the hurt, and the listener repeats their words back to them. For example, the speaker is afraid that the lateness is a sign that his partner has lost interest in him and might leave.

In Step Four, the speaker acknowledges some responsibility for the problem and admits something they could have done differently. For example, the speaker admits he put pressure on his partner to meet him early, even though he knew she had a busy day.

In Step Five, the speaker expresses some understanding of what led the other one to behave as they did. For example, the speaker could acknowledge the fact that his partner has been working long hours lately and feels under pressure.

This may do the trick, but often there is more under the surface and the process may need to be repeated. Or it may stir something in the other partner and they would like to do their own Path to Peace. I watched a couple practise this – they moved from the girl's anger that her boyfriend left the cap off the toothpaste tube, through her feelings about his disregard of her requests, and her fear that his sloppy ways meant he didn't care about her. Within minutes, they reached a reconciliation in which he obviously understood her underlying fears for the first time and they both felt heard and seen by the other.

There is another peace process I came across in *Teachings on Love*, a book by the Vietnamese Zen Buddhist monk, Thich Nhat Hanh. It is longer than the Path to Peace, but it provides a wise and skilful formula within which to express and resolve anger. You can also find it in his book, *Touching Peace*. Thich Nhat Hanh calls it the Peace Treaty, and it is practised at Plum Village, his retreat centre in France. It is too long to quote here, but it begins:

"In order that we may live long and happily together, in order that we may continually develop and deepen our understanding, we the undersigned vow to observe and practise the following."

I like this phrasing because it sets out what is at stake. We would all like to live long and happily with the ones we love most. The most successful couples have arrived at ways of expressing and resolving their differences and, if you haven't working this out already, these two processes may help.

You may read about these techniques and think, "I'm not going to go to all that trouble and make all that fuss. We can sort ourselves out."

You may be right. You and your partner may be naturally sunny and naturally skilled at handling the challenges of anger and disappointment and jealousy. I am not. Most of us aren't, and I know from experience that people who thrash about in the midst of fear and anger are like people struggling in a deep swamp. They get further in themselves, and they are in danger of drawing down anyone who tries to help them.

These peace processes are drawn up by wise people on the high dry ground of compassion and calm. They use these techniques in their own lives when they need to. The processes can be a lifeline to us people in the swamps if we use them well. They are particularly good for people who hate going on about emotions, because they are swift and effective and save days of recrimination and missed communication.

I think to be truly effective these practices need to be introduced in a relationship as early as possible, because no lifeline will save you from an emotional swamp that has deepened over years. Agreeing to use a peace process means that partners are committed to a double awareness of their own behaviour and their partner's feelings. This is living and loving consciously and responsibly, and it is the essence of mature love.

The Joy of Intimacy

Passion is very thrilling, but it is the quiet acts of intimacy that move me to tears. Intimacy reveals itself in small moments of service between one human being and another. It is an intimate act to brush someone's hair or to massage their feet or clip their toenails. It is an intimate act to soothe the knots of tension from someone's neck or to paint their fingernails or to sit together side by side on a sofa, one holding the other's feet in their lap.

It is an intimate act to perch in the bathroom and chat while the other person soaks in the tub. It is an intimate act to scratch someone's back or wash their hair or pluck their eyebrows. It is an intimate act to do for an adult what is unthinkingly and unselfconsciously done for a child – to rub them down after a bath, dry their hair, spoon-feed them, put them to bed.

All of these little acts express tenderness, care, humility and service. They are humble, sweet and nurturing. They pay extreme attention to the receiver, and they absolve them of temporary responsibility. They are unspectacular and they are irresistible. Their repetition silently weaves love into the fabric of everyday life.

Acts of intimacy involve a small surrender of ego on the part of the giver and the receiver. The giver stoops to doing small and quiet things. The receiver allows themself to be vulnerable. This is the opposite of the grand romantic gesture, which inflates the ego of the one who gives and the one who receives. If someone climbs a mountain with roses between their teeth, they become the kind of heroic figure who climbs mountains with roses between their teeth. If someone receives roses from one who has climbed a mountain to bring them, they become the kind of person for whom it is worth climbing mountains. Roses are grand, but sometimes you want the kind of love that buttons the last button you can't reach, or wipes your nose when your hands are busy mending a car or washing dishes.

Everyone should receive a few grand romantic gestures in their life just to know what it feels like to star in your own movie, but true and lasting happiness grows out of repeated acts of intimacy. Gestures are for public view. Intimacy flourishes in the protection of privacy. It is the tender plant that seeds when all the need for preening and pretence is over.

The Joy of Companionship

There was one recurring moment in the routine of my married life that I almost miss the most. It was the point on a Friday night, at the end of a busy week, when my husband and I would sit down together at the table before a bottle of wine, a meal and a pile of the magazines and journals we hadn't got round to reading. Silently, side by side, topping up each other's glasses and replacing the plates, we would sit and read and calm down, doing something we enjoyed, quietly, companionably.

I went to lunch at the house of a friend who had married late for the second time. The couple had known each other in their teens but had grown away and married other people, and then they had refound each other in mid life. Their happiness in their house and garden and in each other was palpable. "Let's face it, Lesley," said the husband, "at our age it's not the sex that's so important, it's the companionship."

Years earlier, as a very young writer, I had gone to interview an elderly couple of writers whose marriage had been famously unfaithful and stormy. Now their chief pleasure, in their eighties, was sitting on opposite sides of their fireside and reading aloud to each other. After infidelity and jealousy, the ultimate reward: companionship.

You may think this is something for the old and doddery, a reward for the slow withdrawal of sexual pleasure, but it isn't at all. I love to spot moments of companionship in the relationships of children, teenagers, even my two cats, who would unite in a blissful tangle at the end of the day, all passion spent. Children love to read side by side, teenagers to mooch aimlessly. This is all done better in companionship than alone.

Who writes about the undramatic pleasures of companionship? It is hard to see what is going on here because, to the naked eye, not a lot is. Companionship is deeper than physical passion or intellectual engagement. It is almost a merging of energies. Companionship comes in those moments when partners are bonded beyond words. They don't need to spell out, demonstrate or negotiate their satisfaction with each other. They are side by side rather than face to face, which means they are looking out at the world, or looking inwards, but not alone.

Companionship is a wonderful gift of love, a reward of peace for all the negotiations and adjustments of temperature. When I am alone I still sometimes spend a Friday night sitting with a glass of wine and catching up with the week, and it is still a pleasure. But between solitary reading and reading in companionship with someone you love, there is all the difference in the world.

Baby Love

When my first child was born I experienced a love more full of wonder than anything I had ever known. I was unprepared for this love and this wonder. I was unprepared, after an exhausting and traumatic labour, to see this person held aloft before me and to notice her eyes wide open, dark and staring fixedly and fiercely at the world. She has never lost that energy and intensity, and I was shocked to realise that I had given birth to someone who was already completely there. I had given birth to a powerful presence.

I was unprepared, when this presence was put into my arms and nuzzled on to my breast, for the power with which she seized my nipple and sucked. I gasped. The force of that instinctive sucking woke up my whole body, sent sensations surging through me from my toes to my head. I was claimed and electrified. Like a power grid I was turned on and surging.

I had a second child and the experience was different. The second time I had the pleasure of anticipating the process because I knew how exciting it would be. I was ready for the drama but, being a very different person, my gentle second daughter slipped elegantly into the world and curled up and went to sleep. I realised this was a very different being, and I had better pay a different kind of attention to her.

First time around I was unprepared for the hours this baby and I would simply sit and stare at each other. I was fixated by her round pink face. Our mutual gaze was a private world. Days would pass in awe and wonder. It was like the intense falling-in-love stage of a romance, where nowhere is more entrancing than your lover's eyes. In this stage of growing intimacy there is no embarrassment, no consciousness of self, only an absorption in the other. We were beginning to orbit each other in an instinctive, ancient dance. She was the new planet to my sun, dependent on me and my radiating love for her very life.

I don't remember now how long this blissful honeymoon lasted. It created a time zone of its own: newborn time. Like the intense period of new adult love, a lot of it was passed in the bedroom, and hours would go by without getting properly dressed. Like the intense period of new adult love, a lot of time was spent in intense physical contact, my arms around the baby, the baby nuzzling at my breast. We had separated at the moment of her birth, but we were still spending long hours as one interdependent creature, a little solar system of our own.

Outside this tiny charmed circle stand people whose feelings are hard to express. The father may feel excluded and judge himself harshly for being childish, or he might not admit or consciously recognise his own jealousy and hurt. Displaced brothers and sisters may frankly ask for the baby to be sent back whence it came and, when that fails, resort to what can turn into a lifetime of jealous tricks and attempts to undermine their rival. The dog and the cat may sulk.

You can't expect the baby to do anything about all these threats to the loving status quo. It is really up to the grown-ups to pay attention to what is going on. Life will never be the same again, but it can be more wonderful.

It can be intensely moving to realise that the couple has become a family. I remember the journey home when my husband came to pick us up, me and our baby, from the hospital. My husband drove and I sat in the unfamiliar back seat, cradling our daughter, wrapped in a white shawl, in my arms. In my emotional postpartum state I could feel that the move to the protection of the back seat was a symbolic as well as a physical one. Tears ran down my face as I held my new child and felt taken care of by my husband.

The shell-shocked look on the face of new parents is due to more than lack of sleep. They are undergoing a seismic change in their world view. The babies have come to teach the couple the biggest lesson in unselfishness they will ever have, and if the couple want to retain the closeness they had as two, they must learn to empathise with, express and adjust to the powerful feelings that they are undergoing. There is a new love in the house and it is bigger, more demanding, more grown-up than anything they have known before.

Parent or Lover?

The novelist Alice Thomas Ellis once said shrewdly that men loved women, women loved children, and children loved hamsters. It's as neat a summary of the frustrations of human relationships as I know, especially as I have yet to meet the hamster that showed any affection to anything. Alice Thomas Ellis encapsulates an uncomfortable truth.

Are you a lover or a parent? You may never know until the time comes to make a choice, and by then it may be too late. I didn't know until I had children that I would be one of those women who put her children first. I remember reading Helen Gurley Brown's seminal book *Having It All*, and snorting when I came to the slender mention she gave to the role of parenthood. "Having it all", in Ms Gurley Brown's book, meant managing a great career and a fabulous man. Children didn't get a look in, even though, as millions of parents could tell you, it's the children that change everything. Helen Gurley Brown's advice was to always put your man first and, if you had children, to continue to put the man first, but this is a counsel of a certain kind of perfection, as any woman torn between the demands of husband and children could tell you.

I found I wasn't very good at being a model wife who put her man first. I found I took the view that children were children, and men were grown-ups and ought to be able to look after themselves, which partly explains why I am no longer married. "Having it all", by the way, is an ideal designed to drive people mad. I am with the wit who said you can have a husband, a career and children, but not all at the same time. If we substitute the words "doing it all" for "having it all", the idea become a lot less attractive, and a lot more truthful.

Are you a lover or a parent? It's a serious question, and it's not only women who cease to put their partners first when their children come along. Some men do it too. I would probably do it differently if I had to do it all again. I wouldn't care for my children any less, but I would pay more attention to my husband's needs. I would compromise a bit more. Because, with all respect to Helen Gurley Brown, we really do want it all – and that includes the children. Children or partner is not a choice anyone ever wants to make, and by the time you realise you are making it, it's too late.

The Love of Children

I was walking through a park recently and a little girl of three or four, in a red coat, suddenly ran across my path to play hide-and-seek behind a bush. I was jolted out of my private thoughts by a sudden sense of recognition. I had a little girl like that. Where was she? A moment of disorientation dissolved into a real body blow of pain. Yes, I had a little girl like that, two in fact, and they've gone for ever. They grew up. Now I have two adult daughters who have homes and lives of their own away from me, and that is the natural order of life and exactly how it should be. But for a moment I swallowed surprising tears and stood on that path and mourned for the little laughing girls I had lost. Absurdly, I suddenly wanted them back.

Parenthood is an extraordinary business. People long for babies, never thinking that they will become children who will be off to school, and then teenagers who will grunt and smoke and go dancing in clubs. You invest all your love in somebody who is guaranteed to set off travelling around the world, to leave home, abandoning you to the empty room and the newly empty life. You know that logically, but the longing for and love of children is a natural anaesthetic that dulls the brain. When my elder daughter was going through her most horrible teenage phase, she sat behind two young women on a bus. One of them was confiding her desire for a baby. My daughter said she felt like tapping her on the shoulder and saying, "Don't do it. It'll only end up like me."

If you're lucky even the teenage horror goes, leaving a charming and fascinating young adult. I've just attended a country wedding, where the bride enchanted everyone in her white dress strewn with red roses, and guests queued up to praise her. But I remember when the bride was expelled from school, and when her despairing mother had her arm in plaster for weeks because she'd lashed out at her daughter in sheer frustration and hit the wall instead.

Having children is an intense, lifelong education in love. It is love with all its faces apart from the sexual. It is certainly sensual. You love delicious little children so much you could eat them all up. It is love at its most joyful and playful, love at its most anxious, love at its most foresighted, love at its most sacrificial, tender and patient.

The loving parent is tested at every turn and must never give up. I have sobbed over babies who wouldn't stop crying and wept over recalcitrant teenagers. I have been angrier with my children than with anyone else in my life. I have looked into the eyes of a murderous thirteen year old while she told me she wanted to kill me, and I wanted to kill her right back. And I've held children in my arms and longed to protect them from everything. And I've snuggled down in a heap with children in front of some daft television programme and not wanted to be anywhere else in the world.

I've despaired when they wouldn't do their homework or practise the piano or clear up their room, and I've thrilled when they've finally passed exams and had proper haircuts and done the washing up without being asked. However grim and grisly the relationship was, or however playful and delicious it was, I've tried to stay constant, because this love is the real love that is for life. They may go away but, in your heart, you never do. That alertness for the cry in the night becomes the alertness for the phone call that says they need you. It is my children who have taught me tolerance and wisdom and patience. It is my children who have taught me that you never give up on love, even when the going gets tough.

And it is my children who taught me what my own parents must have felt and gone through in all those years when I took their love for granted. Only once I had my own children did I understand the passion my mother must have felt for me as a child. And I understood too late the ordeals I put my own parents through: the way I married overseas without them, the night my mother lay beside me while I miscarried my first child, the difficulties of their own they have hidden from me so that I could get on with my own adult life.

The love that flows down from generation to generation, when it flows freely, is the dominant good force in our lives. When it is impeded and deflected, when it is distorted and perverted by cruelty, absence and abuse, then it is the dominant bad force and its destructive effects will affect us all our lives.

The longer I live, the more deeply I understand that it is the love between parent and child that has the deepest and most inescapable influence in our lives. Our many adult love relationships are often subconscious replayings of the emotional drama into which we were born.

The best we can do, in order to be a clear conduit of conscious love for our children and their children beyond them, is to clean up our own well. We can do the work, including therapy if necessary, that clarifies the emotional springs of our own upbringing. We can heal the wounds, if we choose. It is our job to do everything we can to avoid passing on the bad stuff because, despite our best endeavours and the passionate love we bear our children, we will make quite enough original mistakes of our own.

The Enemies of Love

The enemy of love is not the temptation from outside. The enemy is always within. A successful couple has its own immune system. The world is full of diseases, but not everyone falls victim to them. The world is full of temptations, but not everyone is beguiled by them.

Bad habits and unhealthy self-destructive living can undermine our immune systems and make us vulnerable to attack from disease. In the same way, there are bad habits in relationships that create the conditions for turmoil and break-up. Happy people don't leave good relationships, but unhappy dissatisfied ones do.

So the enemies of love are not the attractive work colleague or the sexy fitness trainer, the drinking companions or the mother-in-law. These are just viruses looking, consciously or unconsciously, for something to infect. The enemies of love are the forces within us that make us behave in unloving, neglectful or destructive ways. Neglect and indifference, by the way, are just as powerfully destructive and unloving as abuse and infidelity.

The enemies of love are contempt and the many ways of showing it, habit and the many ways of falling into it, inattentiveness and all the opportunities for intimacy and empathy that it misses. They are bad moods and the corrosive effect these have on other people, jealousy and its insatiable hunger for proofs, anger and its hydra-headed forms, from rage to cold silence.

The enemies of love are constant criticism and its infinite self-justification, nagging and its stupid inability to change tack, constant absence and the growing gulf it creates. They are lying and its destruction of trust, indifference and its irresistible power of erosion. They are unkindness and its deadly ability to wound and never heal, meanness and its stifling of all generosity. I am sure you can think of more.

All of these agents are the real forces of emotional destruction. Where they are uncontrolled, they are the death of love. They work away inside a relationship until all an outsider has to do is to knock at the door for the fortress to be breached. And in case you are thinking, "Yes, I've known people who've behaved like that", think again. I mean you. I mean me.

A sense of self-righteousness can be as big an enemy of love as all the rest. I have often been the agent and perpetrator of my own destruction. And so have you.

Lesley's Theory of Overlapping Circles

There's a mathematical formula somewhere which tells you exactly in what proportion two people's lives have to overlap in order for love to last. I have no idea what it is. I just know it exists.

At first, distance and difference can be a powerful magnetic force. It is very exciting to feel that you have never met anyone like this before. Their very strangeness attracts your attention and their opposition to you somehow completes you. I don't necessarily mean the difference between a European aristocrat who marries a Masai warrior, although these trans-cultural matches are always intriguing. I mean anyone who isn't you.

Other people's worlds can be exotic even if their home is two blocks away from yours. Their life can still be a foreign country where people speak a different language. They butter their bread differently there, and wash the dishes in an idiosyncratic way. They eat different food, have different ways of using the bathroom. They worship a different God. And that's before we get to the very different worlds between their ears.

These early differences have all the charm of an undiscovered country. This new person makes you see everything in a different, foreign light. They can open doors you didn't know existed, and subtly you find your life is changing in ways that, if you are lucky, make you feel more challenged, more alive.

And yet there are small annoyances. You begin to be irked by the way they squeeze the toothpaste tube. Your teasing laughter at their driving or their table manners becomes a little testy. The way they live in a bohemian carelessness that was once so attractive begins to feel more squalid than glamorous. Their habit of being late is slowly becoming inconsiderate rather than the charming evidence of a fully packed life.

These are the little external things. There may be bigger clashes. You thought you loved the great outdoors, but one of you actually likes to camp in it while the other wants to rent a picturesque cottage and gaze at it through the window. You thought you shared a love of good food, but one of you is neurotically demanding about what they eat while the other is easy-going. You thought you were excited about each other's careers, but the careers seem to be forcing you apart. Your overlapping circles are in danger of flying asunder.

It is one of life's challenges that it is possible to love somebody and be driven demented by them at the same time. It is possible to love someone and to realise, slowly and desperately, that your ways of life are incompatible.

It is also possible for people who have very little in common to stay together because they have strong mutual respect, great mutual trust, and because their area of shared interests, though very small, is just enough glue to hold them together. In my experience this even has to be a bit more, alas, than sharing a home and children.

If you feel your overlapping circles sliding apart, it is time to act if you want to save the relationship. The relationship is beyond saving if only one of you wants to do this, because the smallest but most essential common thread must be the mutual desire to stay together come what may. If you don't catch the slide in time, an external gravity begins to take hold which will only pull you farther apart, because the force of attraction is acting more powerfully outside the relationship than in it.

Recognising differences and being honest about them is a start. Genuine willingness to resolve or at least accommodate them is essential. So is willingness to give time to the relationship in order to restore the balance. Nothing will change without a spirit of compromise on both sides, and even with this your relationship may wobble wildly on its axis. As the poet, Yeats, said: "Things fall apart, the centre cannot hold." The Theory of Overlapping Circles had obviously affected him too.

Love versus Space: the New Infidelity

The end of love in the twenty-first century is space. Somehow it's supposed to be less insulting to need your space than it is to criticise your lover. It's not that I find you boring, it's just that I need my space. It's not that I don't fancy you since you put on 10 kilos, it's just that I need some space. It's not that our marriage is over or that I don't want children, it's just that I need some personal space to sort myself out. And once sorted out, how many lovers, wives and husbands return to the narrow confines of the old relationship? Precious few.

Space is the new empire, the new nunnery, the new great excuse. It's where people retreat from love when they don't want to hurt someone, but they end up hurting them anyway – especially if their abandoned partner suspects that space is just another name for the fitness instructor or that new girl at the office. Which it shouldn't be, by the way. Everyone recognises space as the neutral retreating ground. So space is the perfect way to avoid the explosive confrontation that would happen if it really were the fitness instructor.

This is what happens if the need for space gets too desperate. It starts off small and ends up huge. It begins with a night on the sofa and ends on another continent. Space goes from a weekend away alone to a job in another town. Space grows from the garden shed to divorce. If the one you love suggests they need more space, especially if it's a unilateral move, you may not have a crisis on your hands, but it's a warning to pay attention.

In an attempt to neutralise its power, space comes built into relationships these days. How many marriages now begin with Kahlil Gibran's words on love, from *The Prophet*:

Love one another but make not a bond of love:
Let it rather be a moving sea between the shores of your souls…
Sing and dance together and be joyous, but let each one of you be alone.
Even as the strings of the lute are alone though they quiver with the same music.

These words seem to offer a more manageable pattern for a contemporary relationship than the words of the Christian marriage service, with its challenging talk of "for better for worse, for richer for poorer", and its promises to forsake all others. There is nothing there among those solemn words about negotiating space.

Space does have a lot to be said for it. The judicious use of space keeps many relationships going. Space is where you can sleep without being driven mad by snoring. Space is where it is permissible for one partner to go on a painting holiday while the other partner goes fishing. Space is what everyone needs to breathe and recharge. Space, in the right proportion, is what renews energy, appreciation and affection for the other. Space is good because people can choke to death from too much intimacy.

So how can you tell good space – the stuff that allows you to breathe – from bad space, the kind that will simply take your breath away? Good space is negotiated. Bad space is stolen. Good space ends up with two people being pleased to see each other. Bad space just turns into more and more space until your spacious lover disappears over the horizon completely. So when the one you love says they want more space, it isn't necessarily the beginning of the end. But it could be, as Winston Churchill said, the end of the beginning.

How Do You Know When It's Over?

It's over when one of you says it is. It's as cruel and as clear as that. Love may be a consensus, but the end of love is often unilateral. I was reminded of that by the man I was helping to prop up the bar. He was going through a very bitter divorce. His wife had returned to her own country, taking their child with her, and neither the medical nor the legal system would give him any help. Slowly, and very expensively, he was losing both wife and child. I tried to say wise and comforting things, but the fact that his wife had refused all offers of conciliation, marriage guidance and counselling stumped me. She had decided it was over and everything after that was just damage limitation.

The commitment that counts is not the one you make to each other, but the one that both of you make to the relationship. More and more people are choosing not to marry, but the formality of a wedding in the public presence of your friends, family and community makes it very clear that a marriage is something built to overarch the temporary and fleeting feelings of the people within it. It is a structure designed to be visible from within and without, and to shelter its inhabitants from storm and drought, fire and plague. When one partner is down the other holds firm, and the beauty of the public commitment is that the wider community is complicit in this treaty. It is there to be called on when the inevitable difficulties arise.

When a couple disintegrates the shock reverberates. It is not just about them. Parents and siblings are shaken. Loyalties have to be decided. Friendships and social circles can be torn apart. Children, if there are children, have their lives changed forever.

Some couples stay together through enormous, heart-wrenching difficulties. They support each other through sickness and disablement, through poverty and debt, even through cruelty and abuse. If their commitment is to the relationship, they can even survive the trying periods of boredom and dislike. The glue at the centre is stronger than the pull to leave. It can hold together the most unlikely people but, when the end comes, it is often unilateral. It took two people to decide to be together. It only takes one to decide to go, and the couple is through.

The effect on the one left behind can be devastating, but the challenge is to accept reality. If you are the one left behind, whatever you are offering, it is not enough to counterbalance the pull of life outside the relationship. Whatever is in the balance against you – a new partner, a different kind of life, pure freedom – it has won.

It is only natural for this gravity to pull you too. A time of break-up is a time of yearning and loss. It is also a time of anger and revenge. The yearning and the anger are both facets of your attachment to your lost love. They will both hold you in the past if you let them.

Survival at the end of a relationship demands that you identify and express the powerful feelings sweeping through you, but express them in a way that won't cause you or others further damage. Seek therapy if you are struggling on your own. Confide in friends. Above all, try to break the cycle. Beware of rebound relationships or you could find yourself repeating a pattern. Your ultimate goal should be restored self-worth and a new life so satisfying that you no longer care what happens to your lost love. I once met a very successful actress who had enjoyed sweeping past her ex's house in a new Rolls Royce. "Success is the best revenge," she purred.

This is a time to seek out old friends, to re-member your best self. Lost love frees up lots of time. Don't just obliterate it with work or drink or drugs. Take some time to find out what else makes you happy, and explore it. You have time to excavate those parts of yourself that have maybe lain unused in this particular relationship.

Don't expect to go from shock and misery to happiness overnight. Depending on how deep your relationship went, it could take a year or two. But you can create islands of happiness in your sea of despair. And those islands can become stepping stones on to dry land. Dry land is where we look back at the sea of despair and our lost loves like so many boats on the horizon and wonder what we saw in them. Then one day, another boat may come along and, even if we're not ready for an ocean voyage, we can set off for a trip around the lighthouse. We're getting ready to sail again.

When Love Hurts, You See Love Everywhere

It was dark. I was tired at the end of the day and my heart was a raw wound. I sat down in the train carriage and my heart hurt at the sight of the young man and woman who sat across the aisle. They were in love. They couldn't stop touching each other and it made my heart leak tears.

When you are hurt in love and unhappy, the sight of love is intolerable. You are starving. Every look the lovers exchange, every soft touching of a hand or teasing nudge of a foot is a dish in a banquet from which you are excluded. They are in love. You are lonely and nobody is looking at you like that. Maybe they never will again, ever.

The idea that you have become such a damaged and unworthy person that the mere sight of other people's happiness is unbearable only adds to your sense of exclusion. What awful thing is happening to you?

It is a kindness to yourself, when you are in this wounded and highly sensitive state, to remove yourself from these secondary sources of pain. Do not read love stories, go to romantic movies, hang out with friends who are at the self-involved, romantic stage of love. You can choose to do this, of course, if you want to intensify your own feelings and go for broke in the anguish and suffering stakes. But give yourself a break. Seek out friends who are not in the ecstatic throes of love, while avoiding those who are as miserable as you and longing to form a bitter little company of the spurned and rejected. Choose activities and places that will distract and entertain you from your ongoing misery. The pain will catch you unawares quite well without your help.

The ideal state, short of rejoicing in the love of others because you are happily in love too, is one of amused sympathy. You don't want to feel the pain of exclusion that I felt. You don't want to have moved sideways into bitterness and cynicism, to think, "Oh yeah, I was like that once and it didn't last." It is agreeable to think, when confronted by people's love, that it's sort of sweet, without being emotionally affected. Until you can do this at the sight of love in a public place, change your seat, avert your gaze, and make sure you have something to read that will distract you and block the lovers out.

The Chambers of the Heart

The writer Gustave Flaubert fell in hopeless love with an older, married woman and, being a writer, got a book out of it. "Each one of us has in his heart," he wrote, "a royal chamber. I have had mine bricked up but it is still there."

I find Flaubert's book about hopeless love, *A Sentimental Education*, very annoying. His hero lets his life go by as he idealises and moons over the married woman he once saw on a boat. He hardly knows her but he allows her, or the fantasies he has of her, into the royal chamber of his heart, and thereby makes his heart uninhabitable for anyone more suitable.

We all have different patterns of loving which are reflected in the royal chamber of our hearts. Some people have an inbuilt compass which directs them to a healthy love. They find it and cultivate it happily for the rest of their days. Their royal chamber is open and functional. Some people only hang around for the intensely romantic phase of love, and then begin to get restless and in need of the next emotional high. Their royal chamber has revolving doors. Some people are perpetual moths to the flame of unavailable, unattainable lovers, endlessly seeking out the emotional territory of abandonment and blame. Their royal chamber is a war zone with bullet holes in the walls.

If we take the Flaubert model, some hearts must look more like a run-down tenement building than a palace. What I do know is that any heart that is bricked up in honour of the past is in trouble. The challenge, when love is hopeless or gone, is not to brick up your heart and turn it into a mausoleum. It is to change the locks, redecorate the walls, and put up a To Let sign.

How do you do that? I am not the best person to ask. I have a sad tendency to cling on hopefully because I hate to see something good go bad. I also – writer, only child – have a higher tolerance of my own company than many people. I am not driven mad by the single state – at least, only intermittently – so my motivation for getting out into the market place again is not as high as it might be. However, I would hate to think I have a bricked-up heart. It's just that my To Let sign isn't as prominent as it might be.

If you can't quite bring yourself to throw past loves out of your heart lock, stock and barrel, perhaps the first thing to do in letting go is to move them into mental storage. Take the evidence of their role in your life – which can be real like photographs, clothes and books – and put it all in a box and close the lid. Bravo to those who dump all this on their ex's doorstep, but your state may be more sorrow than anger and you might not be ready to go this far. In your heart you label this box The Past. Cry if you must. Imagine closing a heavy door on it. In real life, if you can't get to the dump, put the box where you can't see it. Re-visit it in six month's time. Re-visit it until it means nothing and you can give it away. This might take years and, for some people who like being surrounded by the detritus of their emotional life, it may never happen.

I once had a favourite T-shirt I associated with a particular boyfriend. It was my lucky T-shirt and I always wore it when I went on planes because the happiness it contained held the plane up. The affair lasted months. The aftershock lasted two years, but it was five years before I packed a suitcase and left the T-shirt behind. It took one more year before I threw it out altogether. I told you I was slow to let go.

However long it takes to get rid of the physical evidence, you should have created a space in your life and in your heart. Clean and clear it out some more. Write a letter to your lost love telling them exactly, truthfully, vengefully if you must, what you think and feel about them. Put it all in – the anger, the hurt, the lost hope, the gratitude, the pain and regret. Burn the letter. Write another one. Burn it again. Keep writing till the energy lightens and the charge has gone.

Now write an advertisement for your heart. Word it your way, but draft it along these lines:

Heart to let. Perfect residence for right tenant. Ideal family home or luscious love nest. Flat sharers welcome (or not). Recently refurbished to highest standard. Short lets only or long lease available. Viewing by appointment only. References required.

Are you ready to let people know that your heart is available? Maybe not, in which case carry on furnishing it. Close your eyes and imagine walking around it. What can you see from the windows? Describe the furnishings, the books, the artworks, the music you can hear. Is there room for a new occupant or is it overstuffed with out-of-date furnishings? If you can see that your previous tenant has sneakily moved back in be ruthless. Change the locks. Write more letters.

You may not feel ready for a new long-term tenant, but is there any harm in showing one or two people around? You don't have to give anyone the key. In the meantime, keep re-visiting, keep re-furnishing. You want to fill it with things you love. And you can have anything – loot the world's museums, commission the finest artists. It's your heart. It may have been trashed by the previous tenant, but you can turn it back into a palace.

And all the time you are doing this you are creating a pathway to your heart, a vivid new connection with the world. With a royal chamber like this, full of music, colour, light, could you ever again let in anyone who would trash it?

Now describe your ideal tenant. They'd treat your heart with respect wouldn't they, or why would you let them in? They might want to move in some of their own furnishings, and store some of yours, but with mutual care and respect this can be an exciting process. You'd want to know a little bit about them before you handed over the keys. Do they have good references? People can move on for perfectly good reasons, but you want to know that they will take good care of your heart. I can't guarantee you magical results, but I can guarantee that this imaginative process will teach you a lot about yourself, and be fun. If the royal chamber of your heart is bricked up, this is a gentle way to take the bricks down again.

How to Stay Married for Sixty Years

We were planning a special lunch for my parents' diamond wedding anniversary in a lovely country hotel. My eighty-four-year-old father and I had gone in to view the room, pick the champagne, choose the food. Then my mother fell ill and went into hospital, so the event was postponed.

On the eve of the anniversary my father rang me at half past ten at night. "I've been thinking," he said, "that tomorrow I will have been married to your mother for sixty years, and it seems quite wrong to go and visit her in hospital in the afternoon as if it were just a normal day. I want to get up and go straight there in a taxi first thing in the morning. What do you think?"

"Quite right," I said, even though, for the last six months, my father has been housebound with the multiple afflictions of the elderly, and spends most of his mornings in bed. "It's time for a grand romantic gesture."

And so my father, who is rarely up and fully dressed before noon, rose, washed, shaved and dressed before nine o'clock. He then set off in a taxi to the hospital, where my eighty-one-year-old mother was marooned with pancreatitis. There he told her, in the setting of a public ward, for the umpteen thousandth time, how much he loved her.

On the brilliant May day on which they married in an English country church sixty years before, my giddy exuberant young parents had known each other for less than six weeks. It was wartime, 1944, and he was a twenty-four-year-old flight lieutenant in the RAF and she was a young member of the WAAF. He fell for her as soon as he saw "this delicious little thing". A day later he asked her to marry him and she laid her head on his chest and said, "Thank you very much, but no." A couple of weeks of persistence, poetry and relentless charm later she said, "Ask me again." So he did and she said yes. When he asked her why she'd changed her mind she said, "You're good looking, you're clever and you've got a good degree and I'm a bit of an intellectual snob." They were married a week later by special licence from the Bishop of Salisbury. Well, it was wartime.

There was no time to meet each other's families, although my uncle got leave from the army long enough to give my mother away. My father was married in his uniform and my mother in a smart little suit, and their honeymoon night was spent in a nearby seaside hotel.

On the day of their diamond wedding anniversary, sixty years later, the weather was just as glorious as it had been all that time ago. When I took my father back to my mother's hospital ward that afternoon, we carried cards and presents and a cake and an aromatic posy of flowers. We sat outside the ward in a sunny courtyard and wondered how it was they'd stayed together all these years.

My father, who is a writer whose hands have become disablingly crippled with arthritis, had begun his day by opening his long-abandoned journal. "On this day, sixty years ago," he wrote, in his arthritic spidery writing, "I had the great good fortune to be married to Wendy." When I said, "Go on, Dad, what's the secret?" he thought for a second and then said emphatically, "Luck."

Well, there is an element of luck in marrying somebody you've only known for six weeks and finding out, over sixty long years, that you haven't married an axe-murderer, but someone infinitely loving, good and kind. My mother, naturally, thought there was more to it than that. "It's never considering that there's an alternative," she said. "It's being able to be very cross with each other but never falling out," said my dad. "And always having interesting things of your own to do so you're not just dependent on each other," added my mother.

All of these things are true. I have my own point of view, the unique and privileged view of an only child. In this triumvirate I am the perpetual witness and also often the recipient of both the loving and the critical confidences of each parent about the other.

"Your father is a very trying man," sighs my mother, but she is still lovingly willing to be tried. "Your mother is very impetuous and headstrong," grumbles my father, and goes on to mutter that, although everyone thinks my mother is sweet and saintly, she actually has a very nasty temper, which I know is true.

And they confide the good things too. "Your father is a very remarkable man," says my mother. "Your mother is a very good kind person," says my father, who is much less forgiving and sociably inclusive than she is.

Sometimes, as the recipient of a moment of exasperation or frustration, I have made the great mistake of trying to act as the advocate for the temporarily disgruntled one. But it only serves to have them unite against me. I will be told that nobody is as close as they are, nobody more lovingly partnered, that if I think either one of them is being unkind or inconsiderate to the other then I don't understand the unique nature of their relationship. I shut up.

This is what I observe, as the sole product and lifelong witness of this uniquely close and constantly lively partnership. It is a relationship where there are few moments of silence. These two people find each other constantly interesting. They talk continuously, about the state of the world, about what they are reading or watching on television, about what they should eat for dinner or plant in the garden. They enliven this non-stop dialogue by bickering and arguing, but are upset if anyone should mistake this sparring for a genuine row. They disagree constantly. They each have a great respect for the other, but they each also have a great respect for themselves and their opinions, and defend them vigorously. They also love each other very much, and their most heated arguments take place when one is convinced that they know exactly what is best for the other.

There is a tidal flow to this constant, uninterrupted interchange. Sometimes it is heated argument and barbed frustration. Sometimes it is quiet and tender, and expresses itself in a soft kiss, a hug or a gentle pat on the hand or cheek. My mother tries to remove the obstacles from my father's path. My father tries to rein my mother in and stop her from over-running or exhausting herself. When either one is down, the other quivers with sympathetic anxiety. In moments of relaxation or holiday they are still quintessentially youthful. In their eighties, they still have an intellectual brightness, a vivacity, a humour that made them irresistible when they were young, vigorous, good looking and full of bounce.

There have been difficult and trying times in my parents' lives, periods of crisis and illness and drama. But neither of them ever gives up, not on life, not on the problem, not on each other. They are good at remembering to appreciate each other. My mother always looks immaculate and wonderful, and my father is always proud that she does. My mother is often dumbstruck by my father's ingenuity, resourcefulness and sheer brain power.

Some battles they will never win. My father says that in sixty years my mother has never let him finish a sentence. My father, over sixty years which must mean at least twenty thousand dinners, has never failed to drive my mother demented by disappearing somewhere just as the hot food is set on the table. But he also never fails to appreciate the food and tell her how good it is. I have seen my mother fly at my father in 5 foot of unleashed fury, and I have seen my father draw himself up to his full 6 feet and say, his voice tight with resentment, that he will never forgive her for whichever affront she has committed. But she calms down and he does forgive her. Nothing is irrevocable, the sweetness always returns.

My daughter, their granddaughter, says that my mother told her that they had been through plenty of things that other people might have got divorced over, but they never did. "It's a shame," says my daughter, "when you look at all the people who get divorced and who won't ever know what it's like to be together for so long like Mum and Bill."

What is it like? It is to be half of a lifelong dialogue. It is to be quite separate, strong-willed, highly individual people whose utter commitment to each other, through weariness, rage, despair, intense irritation, illness, breakdown, is completely non-negotiable. I can't imagine they have ever wasted a minute talking about whether to separate, although they may have spent hours, days, talking about how to get through the next stage together. It is to be two opposing poles, forever repelled, forever drawn to each other. It is to be two people more stricken by anxiety for the other than by thought for themselves. It is to be two people who would never, ever let the other down, say goodnight without tenderness, or leave without a parting kiss. It is to be two people fiercely driven by what is right for the other. It is to be two people in an indivisible, impenetrable whole. And it is to be two people who are an endlessly renewable source of loving care and forgiveness for each other.

It has been some years since my father admitted to me that they had reached the stage of life where they each wake in the morning and listen to hear if the other is still breathing. The angel of death has hovered around a few times, darkening our lives with the shadow of fatal wings, before flapping off again without landing this time. I strongly suspect that he found my parents, even in age and sickness, too deep in their sixty-year-long exchange of challenge, care and concern to pay him the right sort of attention.

Making an Audit of Love

This is my audit of love. I am alone. I am alone in a room. I am alone in a house. I am alone in a street. On this particular day I would have to walk a long way to find another human being whom I could touch or whom I could expect to touch me.

There is nowhere I could find any sexual excitement or comfort. I could find some social kisses and hugs within a mile or so. I'd have to travel 10 miles across town for a genuine cuddle. On the map of my country there are places where I would find a loving hug, but some of them are hundreds of miles away. Across the channel in Europe I could find some hugs and kisses too but, for this morning, I'll have to imagine them.

What – alone in a room, alone in a house, alone in a street – can I do to experience the feelings of connection, nourishment, affirmation, *joie de vivre* that come with love?

Obviously, immediately, I can use the telephone. When I land on my home planet after a long journey, as I did yesterday, I reconnect myself by means of the human voice. There are essential people – daughters, ex-husband, friends, cousins, parents – that I need to reconnect with to feel securely repositioned in my world. I want them to know where and how I am. And I need to know where and how they are. I need, for my own sense of emotional wholeness, to learn their news, laugh with them, listen as they share their successes, unravel their anxieties. Their familiar voices over the telephone have a physical effect on me that email never has. I am calmed as I feel myself reweaving the pattern of my life with my emotional tribe, as I knot another thread in my emotional web.

But I am still alone in a room, alone in a house, alone in a street. Returning from a journey I feel the lack of a friendly voice, welcoming arms, a hand to lift my luggage or make me a cup of tea or a meal. Love as emotional drama may hog the headlines, but it is love as the quiet engine of daily life that I miss when I return from sharing other people's houses to the quiet solitude of my own.

So I unwrap one of the great gifts of solitude – reflection. And with reflection comes awareness. In the hurly-burly of a collective emotional life there is no time to think, to sort and evaluate. I've just spent several days in a house with twelve people who ranged from sixty years old to fifteen months. There was constant closeness, a lot of laughter, busyness, activity, much connecting, but not a moment to think. Alone again I take time to think in the best way, not in the circular obsessive path that thoughts can follow if the thinker is too much alone, but in a directed and orderly way.

Alone in a room, in a house, in a street, with time at my disposal, I am going to make a personal audit of love. I am going to tally my assets, catalogue my debits. I want to come to a true understanding of my emotional wealth and poverty. I want to see what capital I can draw on. I want to see how to repay my debts, how to build on my assets, what gives me pleasure to spend, what risks I could take.

I lift my eyes from the page and in the mirror on my mantelpiece I see I have stuck two cards. One is a thank you note from a friend who stayed with me one weekend and shared confidences. The other is a photograph I took, in the green hills of Iceland, of a stream that ran with hot water. The picture of the stream curving through the green meadow reminds of the day when five of us jumped into its steaming waters and floated there, laughing and singing, with the green grasses and wildflowers stretching away at eye level, sharing pure magic.

Propped against the mirror is a small photograph of a bearded man in Afghan dress flanked by two bright-eyed little girls in summer frocks and Afghan socks. The man is my former husband, Ken, on the day he returned from a medical aid mission to Afghanistan, travelling in local dress with the Mujahadeen at the time of the Russian occupation. He was so thin when he returned that we didn't recognise him at the airport. This is one of my favourite photographs, layered with memories, and what makes it extra special is that, one Mother's Day, the girls took it away and decorated it with a collage of cut-out leaves and flowers, with the word "Mum" in the top left-hand corner. The flowers obscure the photograph, but I wouldn't remove them for the world.

There are more things on my mantelpiece: a handful of pebbles from a Greek beach, a wooden carving of two birds in a tree that I fell in love with, a tiny wooden angel that came as a gift. There's a fig-scented candle I was given at Christmas, and a bottle of my favourite fig-based perfume which everyone loves when I wear it.

Wherever I look in my bedroom, the room with me alone in it, I feel less and less alone. My bedroom is a harbour full of anchors that tether people, memories, connections to other places and other times. Names come to mind, and recollections, as my eye travels the room. Elaine gave me that lap-desk, the children that clock radio. I bought those stones from Daryl, that Venetian glass necklace from Valerie. I was with Marianna when I found that little lamp, with Deidre and Susie on Crete when I bought the green glass bird. My digital camera on the shelf is a magic box of collected love: images of David and Daryl's house in the snow, Mel and Rhiannon at the kitchen table, Harriet, Ken and Alistair fooling around in the lighthouse kitchen, Rachel cooking me a meal. The room is all presence, not absence.

There's a stack of CDs that I love on the floor. On the wall is my favourite painting: a little family group on a beach a hundred years ago, the love and affection washed on to the paper in the artist's curving brushstrokes, capturing the familiar, embracing gestures of his wife and child.

This is all I can see at a glance. I haven't opened a cupboard door or pulled out a drawer to find the evidence of love stored inside. I haven't left this one room to enter another to explore the freight of love that each object in my house brings, or to wonder why I still house that furniture, those books, those things that bring no love with them.

Not alone in a room. Not alone in a house. Maybe not alone in a street. From my bedroom window I can see the pot plants in my neighbour's window. Terry across the road puts my garden in order and gardens his own with love. I may see the blank grey front wall of his house, but I know that hidden at the back is a private urban jungle, mysterious and magical with exotic trees and shrubs. Between us, the maple tree on the pavement before my house is coming into pink striped leaf, bringing me my summer screen of thick leaves. I love this tree for its beauty, its luxuriance, for the blue tits, jays and magpies that visit it, for its summer screen of privacy.

Not alone in a room. Not alone in a house. Not alone in a street. I put the audit to one side, with its overloaded columns of credit. The act of beginning it has brought my attention completely to a sense of fullness and privilege. A loved one, the One, the elusive One we all seek, may be absent, but the presence of love is everywhere if I stop to read the signs.

Friendship Is Forever

Exclusive love comes and goes, but if you pay attention to them your friends are always there. I love my friends. My friends are my family, my travelling companions, my flat mates, my security blanket, my safety net, my partners in heartbreak and adventure and in all kinds of fun.

My friends are my memory too, and the witnesses of who I am. We look out for each other. I have a friend called Peter. We met across a garden fence when I was two years old, bit each other and bonded. Peter was sixty this year. He's a grandfather, a professor, a sober citizen in every way. For his sixtieth birthday party I read him a poem I'd written which began, "Peter had a sandpit". He was deeply moved because he'd forgotten he once had a sandpit. Peter and I don't see each other very often, and there are whole swathes of each other's lives we have missed altogether, but we share memories of childhood that nobody else in the world has. We know that for this very reason our decades-long friendship is a remarkable and precious thing.

When I was in the most active part of my dating life, in my teens and twenties, it was far more common to focus on any love interest that came along and ditch your friends. It was considered acceptable, even desirable and natural, to cancel a date with a girlfriend in favour of a promising man. The women's movement made a big difference to that. Female friendship isn't second best any more. It seems to demand as much time and as much social respect as any romantic relationship. I watch girls in their twenties now balancing girlfriends and boyfriends, and they don't make the huge mistake of putting all their social eggs in one teeny basket. They know that boyfriends will come and go, but girlfriends go on forever if you look after them right.

Once I was in a very intense relationship, or at least, I was in a relationship with a very intense person. There was no room for other friends in our closed world, which at the time was fine by me. Then I began to notice that when he went away on business trips I got to catch up with all my old abandoned friends again, and I had more fun. The relationship ended when I spent the day with my friends and realised I didn't want to go back into my lonely couple-cocoon again.

There's nothing you can't do with your friends except have sex. Apart from that one thing, you can travel with them, live with them, eat and drink with them, play sports with them, go on long walks with them, call them when you're happy, commiserate with them when you're not, help them when they're sick or broken hearted, and ask them for help in return, go dancing with them, get drunk with them, go for years without seeing them and then catch up just where you left off. It's been one of the joys of my life that I have reconnected with close friends I lost touch with in the married, bringing-up-children years, and found that the bond was still so strong I might have seen them yesterday.

The best possible relationship would be one where you felt deep friendship and had good sex too. I do know marriages and relationships like that, and I envy them and wish them well. But a huge amount of the happiness in my life comes from friendship because friends are really people relating to each other in the best possible way. It's a shame about the sex, but you can't always have everything all at once.

Singles and Their Habitat

When you are young and surrounded by people your own age, potential partners are everywhere. Later on you have to work harder. In the interests of research for this book I took myself off to a weekend workshop on relationships run by Seanna McGee and Maurice Taylor, authors of *The New Couple*. It was for singles, and I had worked out before I went that the girls would outnumber the men by quite a lot, though the workshops are for both sexes and men do go. I have learned from experience that most British men would rather have root-canal work done than spend more than five minutes talking about relationships and emotions. When I found that this workshop coincided with a major football match, then I didn't expect to see any men at all – and I was right.

But the other girls on the workshop were disappointed. They thought they might meet someone. Well, we all learned a lot about how to make relationships work that weekend. We learned about anger and how to express it healthily. We learned how to listen, and we learned how to value ourselves so highly that we could set conditions for our future relationships. If you want to know more about what we learned, I suggest you get Seanna and Maurice's book. What we didn't really learn, although it was what concerned us all, was where to find our future soul mates.

If you are a man, you need to know that there were twenty-five women there that weekend, all attractive, all bright, all available. Wouldn't it have been worth giving up a weekend of your time for an opportunity like that? Especially as these women were learning some skills that could prevent a lot of grief in any future relationship. And if not that particular workshop, well, any other workshop would do. The world of personal development is a world where women always seem to outnumber men.

If you are a woman looking for a man, you could learn from a girl called Rosie, who was also on this workshop and said she often meets men playing golf, although she met her latest date through work. And I bet that, if you could have attracted their attention, there were plenty of men at that major football match. If you are going to find fault with this line of thinking, you could argue that you don't want to date the kind of girl who hangs out in personal growth workshops, nor do you want the kind of man who spends his time playing or watching sport. But women are interested in emotions and are more open to self-improvement than men, just as more men are interested in sport – of course there are plenty that aren't, but we're talking averages here. It wasn't because I loved cricket that I volunteered to make the teas at cricket matches when I was at school. It was because I was interested in boys, and there they were. And there they still are, decades later.

Once you are out of higher education and into a world limited by workplaces and working hours, it becomes a lot more difficult to find people to love. Internet chatlines and dating services have mushroomed to serve generations of single people who are chained to their computers. It seems there is a higher chance of meeting somebody in cyberspace than there is of meeting a real, available person in a local bar or at a party. After all, there are millions of people out there in cyberspace, and there are the same old people you already know at your local bar.

Nevertheless, for your own sense of self-worth and amusement, and for increasing your chances of meeting somebody you like, the old advice still applies. Just get out more. I had a very entertaining day recently when I went to the races. There were lots of amusing men, and

I came home slightly better off than I went. I was at an art gallery opening last night and it was packed with single people in their twenties and thirties. A year's membership to the art gallery guarantees me a lot of invitations like that, and I get to learn a lot more about art, which improves my whole quality of life. I didn't meet anybody to love at the opening, but I did go home in a really good mood.

Everyone has to eat, so bars and restaurants and supermarkets are on most people's trajectory. And everyone has to work. The workplace, both statistically and in my experience, is where most people meet, which is why I'm a bit baffled by efforts to cut down romance in the workplace. If not there, then where? And if you want to up your chances, try to find a job in a place where there are plenty of members of the opposite sex. For example, as a young journalist I learned fast that the offices of women's magazines are full of women, whereas newspapers have far more men around. Simple really. If you're a girl, work on a newspaper. If you're a man, try women's magazines.

The secret of happiness, though, is to think bigger than the desperate search to find somebody. You have to do things you enjoy.

You have to do things that improve your quality of life, whether or not you are sharing it with anybody. And if your enjoyable life leads you to a partner that's a bonus.

The Power of Touch

I was having a massage in an Irish spa, and the young Irish masseuse was telling me about her training. "Massage was my favourite, you know," she said dreamily, "because we'd work on each other. So we'd learn to give a massage, and then we'd take turns and receive one while the other learned. It's the affection of it."

I lay under her hands and silently agreed. How can you express the affection of it? We are often starved of affection, but it can be restored by a skilful human touch. And the fact that you pay money for a good massage doesn't mean that the only exchange is commercial. If you get someone who is really good at their job, money can buy you love.

I grew up in and now live in an Anglo-Saxon society in which touch is reserved and slightly suspect. I'm glad that we are all a lot looser than we used to be. We hug, embrace, kiss more freely – even the men, especially if sport is involved. But in other ways we have become more self-conscious and restrained. The awareness of child abuse and the threat of a claim of sexual harassment have done a lot to make people inhibited about reaching out to one another in physical ways. The natural instinct to comfort a child with an encircling arm is curbed. Physical affection is in danger of becoming restricted to consenting adults only. But physical affection – the casual touch, the gentle stroke, the hug, the unselfconscious holding of hands, the ruffling of hair – is the natural, unforced expression of love.

We need to be touched as much as we need to breathe and eat. Children and animals and women who are held and stroked thrive better than those who aren't. It helps the production of oxytocin. It's not quite so important for men apparently, because their hormonal make-up is different. I never thought about this until I met an older, divorced woman who told me that she booked herself a full body massage every week, because now she lived alone she needed to be touched. Even people who live in relationships, and have an averagely happy sex life, rarely experience the ritualistic soothing and re-membering of the body that a good massage can bring. Those rarely touched places, like the spot between the shoulder blades or the tender soles of our feet, can be awakened and calmed and joined in to the rest of us until we are a whole body again, feeling reunited within ourselves, like a child. Ah, the affection of it.

It's the power of touch that women experience at the hairdresser and the manicurist, and which men enjoy at the barber. It's the power of touch that sends little boys wrestling each other like bear cubs, and grown men into contact sports. It's the power of touch that is expressed in grooming. It is the power of touch that makes household pets so valuable to us, pulling our pain out of us with each stroke of a warm furry body. It's the power of touch that makes hand-holders out of little girls and lovers – and, in countries where the open expression of physical affection between men and women is not allowed, out of men. In Arab, African and Asian countries grown men, friends, often hold hands freely in the street, and it is charming.

What makes affectionate touch so powerful is that it demands nothing. It only gives. Sexual touch is powerful, of course, but it has an agenda, it has a goal, and it can lead to pain as well as pleasure. We have become too sexualised as a society to appreciate that everyone needs the touch of a hand that soothes rather than arouses. The only agenda of affectionate touch is the receiving of comfort, and the gentle easing of tension and the giving of pleasure. I've learned that the times when there is no toucher in my life are bearable if I find someone, like my Irish masseuse, who can tell my body it is loved and cared for. Ah, the affection of it.

The Benevolent Crowd

Love is not a self-renewing resource. It must be nurtured and replaced. If I want to give love in the world I must also feed on love. I have to feel love's energy renewing me, if I am not to become a dried-up depleted source. I need to feel love in order to feel alive, and I need to feel love in order to pass it on.

I can do this in many ways, and the couple is only one. It is not enough to sit alone in a room. The telephone, email, text are useful means but not ends. A human being needs physical contact with other human beings, and we need emotional contact too. If I am feeling cut off, isolated or lonely, I know that I will be renewed in a benevolent crowd.

The benevolent crowd is where we feel collective emotion. The uplift of collective emotion is huge. It can transform lives and send spirits soaring. It can inspire and transfigure you. You can find the power of collective emotion in a benevolent crowd at a classical or rock concert, in a sporting stadium, at the theatre, the ballet, the opera, in a dance club, at a racecourse, an athletics track, a revival meeting or a political rally.

Try to choose well. The crowds at the Nuremberg rallies probably felt uplifted, inspired and benevolent, but they weren't. Any crowd magnifies emotions because you are plugging in to a huge source of collective energy, so be choosy about your benevolent crowd and its aims. You want to feel filled with a love of humanity, not with hatred of an enemy. And when you let your boundaries drop, as you do in a benevolent crowd, you don't want to be invaded with the destructive forces that are unleashed in malevolent crowds. What you want is to feel good to be alive. What you want is to feel ecstatic and renewed.

When I talk about finding love I'm talking about the loss of ego, the separate self, in something bigger, whether it is a couple, a family, a football club or a whole nation. The individual who has been swept away in a collective love has the same ecstatic disbelieving look on their face as the intoxicated lover: flushed, bright-eyed, slightly unfocused, their attention turned inward to the recollection of something marvellous. But in the benevolent crowd it is not a lover this emotion is drawn from; it is a rock band, a charismatic speaker, a fabulous sporting performance.

The benevolent crowd meets somewhere every week near you. Join it and it will make you feel human again, but ask some questions first. In selecting when and where to merge, to lose the ego, the same rules of safety apply to crowds as apply to individuals. Is this crowd safe? Will it do me no harm? Will it involve me in addictive behaviours? Silly clothes? Vast expense? A commitment I don't want to make? The risk is smaller than with an individual because the commitment is much smaller too. You can always walk away from a crowd. But if you are in the middle of a benevolent crowd that is having the time of its life doing something elevating, dazzling, harmless, human, then you have seen another face of love and it will make you feel wonderful.

Tracking the Signs of Love

I never stop looking for love. It's just that I look for it in different places now. I've just been on a fungi hunt on a nearby common with two friends and a small dog called Lily. Between the three adults we had three noses, three pairs of eyes, two sets of glasses, a camera, a book about fungi with coloured photographs, and a collective memory of what fungi looked like. The dog had much sharper senses than we did, but no focus on fungi at all. Her only contribution to the hunt was to appear when we were excitedly gathered around a find and walk all over it in her attempt to see what we were looking at.

At first we couldn't find any fungi at all. We trampled through bracken and heather and around the roots of birch and oak trees. We mistook fallen leaves for mushrooms and stones for puffballs. Very slowly the bigger fungi came into focus through the static of visual information that surrounded them. It was autumn and it seemed as though the ground, littered with dried grasses and fallen leaves, was the perfect camouflage for fungi.

But we knew what fungi looked like and we began to single them out. Our eyes grew sharper and our success rate soared. We were developing acute fungi focus. Dead logs sprouted them. Curly orange caps and tiny fairy stalks stood out among the birch leaves. The little purple plates of the Amethyst Deceiver punctuated the grass stalks. What we were learning to do, as we scanned the ground, was to be highly discriminating. We were screening out everything that wasn't fungus, and it worked.

I think I've been like that as I have written this book. I know that developing a focus creates its own screening device, and it works best when it works in this negative way. As far as looking for love is concerned, this means that my antennae are simply refusing to see anything that isn't love. This doesn't mean looking for people to fall in love with. It means recognising that the behaviours of love have a common pattern and are there to be seen if you look for them.

Looking for love in a crowded city means screening out a huge amount of deceptive visual information. Once your focus is working, the evidence of love just leaps out at you. I caught a glimpse of a little girl of around twelve wrapping her arms around an old man even smaller than she was. They were like lovers. Their laughter and their look of unashamed fondness, grandparent to grandchild and back, was love incarnate.

I saw a man struggling to manoeuvre another man in a wheelchair on to a bus and failing, and as he failed, three or four men rushed to help him, without thought or calculation. It was a spontaneous moment of love in action, of the human instinct to help the helpless.

The behaviours of love are spontaneous and inclusive. They involve an act of reaching and enfolding. They show tenderness of expression and gesture. They are utterly undiscriminating and uncritical. They flow between the old and the young, between black and white, between men, women and children. They never seek to control or belittle. They express a joy in life and a pride in the individual.

If you develop this focus it gives you a sharp eye for pseudolove, and you need it because fake love is everywhere. You see it in politicians kissing babies – or their wives. You see it in celebrities, draped over each other for the benefit of the cameras or for career advantage. You see it in public situations where people are putting on a good front, a front that can hide bitterness, division or even indifference. You see it where people criticise and belittle each other in front of others.

The focus gives you a perceptive eye for love gone wrong. It homes in on unkindness and bad temper. It picks up the children being browbeaten or scolded by their parents in public. It can't help registering the negative space between a couple who have had a row or who have simply run out of things to say to each other.

It is fun to put on your spectacles and go out on a love hunt. And it is very educational. It is fun because these little love scenes that get played out under our noses all the time are moving, amusing and life enhancing. And it is educational because we need to develop the antennae that distinguish between the real and the fake. In real life, look-alike love isn't good enough. In fungi, a close resemblance can disguise the fatal gap between life and death. In love, the difference between fake and truth disguises the gap that separates pain from real grown-up happiness.

Set Your Compass to Love

What is your inner compass set to? Are you aware of having an inner compass at all, or are you helplessly buffeted by the wind and weather of emotion, the victim of external forces from the moment your feet touch the ground in the morning to the moment you embrace the dark of night?

Try setting your compass to the true north of love. When your eyes open at daylight, do you love what or who you see? Do you love the face on the pillow beside you? If you do, lucky you. If not, why are they in your bed at all?

If you are the only person in your bed, do you love your sheets? The colour of your walls? The objects on your bedside table? The pattern of your curtains or the view from your window? If the answer is no, you might feel a bit depressed. It might be difficult to change the person in your bed or the view from your window, but it is not at all difficult to change your curtains or your sheets. Once you start to make a conscious choice and choose things that you love, a profound change can be set in motion.

William Morris said we should not have anything in our homes that we do not find to be useful or believe to be beautiful. Here is my counsel of perfection. Do not have anything in your life that you do not love.

Make love the most over-used word in your vocabulary. Let it kick out routine and habit. When you get dressed in the morning, do you love your underwear, your shoes, your fragrance, your ties, your clothes? Did you buy them because you loved them or because you're stuck wearing a uniform, or because you thought they were cheap or inoffensive or useful and would cover your lumpy bits? Do you love the way they make you feel, or do they make you feel comfortably invisible?

Do you love what you eat for breakfast or is it a mindless habit? Do you have an activity you love to look forward to at the end of the day, or do you watch television? Do you really love watching television? Do you love your neighbourhood or is it just handy for transport?

You get the idea. Every single waking moment of our lives offers us choices we can exercise through love, and the simpler the choice the easier it is to make it with love. We can choose to build love from the ground up, instead of grasping it out of some future sky.

I love fresh flowers. I love the bunch of daffodils I bought for less than a pound, which sits in a blue jug I love, on the faded tablecloth I love because I bought it on holiday, spread on the wooden table I love because I fell for the grain and sheen of its surface. This cumulation of simple objects kick-starts my day each morning.

My act of love is the act of attention that takes each object in and acknowledges its place in my life. I can swallow a bowl of cereal inattentively or I can sit at my table and enjoy it slowly, appreciating the blue-rimmed china bowl I eat it from, enjoying the company of my jug of daffodils, and the view of the clump of bamboo in my garden which I can see bending in the morning wind. I love the bamboo and the way it dances. I love the fact that I planted it from a pot and it is now a little grove of stems that give me shade in summer.

If there are people at my breakfast table I can grunt at them from behind the newspaper, which I admit I often do, or I can perform that act of attention, of gratitude, that consciously takes in their presence, listens to what they say, gives thanks for their company. If I have started my day with love I have a small head-start on the brutal forces of indifference and chaos that wait for us all. And I have also tuned myself to recognise and experience love in the confusion and variousness of the day ahead. If my inner compass is set to love, I may get lost a thousand times, but it will always guide me home.

Love Grows Things

I can see my mother among the pots of flowers in her garden. My mother tends her pots lovingly which is why she is surrounded by healthy flowers. She waters them. She notices as soon as a bloom has withered and is turning brown, and she deadheads the dying flowers so that her plants flourish. Even when she is ill and it tires her, she can't leave her garden alone. She will stoop and bend, even though it fatigues and pains her, to pull out strong weeds or depleted bulbs. Her garden bursts with flowers because my mother pays attention to every corner and every plant. She loves them and so they grow.

Things and people that are loved flourish. That is how you can tell. Children that are loved bloom in health and happy self-confidence. Unloved children bear the marks of their neglect or oppression. They look dark or pinched. They are closed in, and sometimes they take out their anger and suffering on others who are weaker than they are. I watched a little girl at a bus stop beating her own doll. "Shut up, shut up, shut up," she repeated grimly as she hit it. Where did she learn such unloving behaviour? In the same place, I imagine, as the little girl who lovingly tucks up her doll, feeds it imaginary food and covers it with tender kisses. In the home.

Love grows things. The older I get the less I want to buy or eat food that isn't grown or prepared with love. I could poison myself with industrially grown and prepared food, which will affect my health for the worse while it makes profits for some giant corporation. Or I can seek out markets, gardens and farms, where producers take a personal pride in their produce, where organically grown vegetables have life and flavour in them, and the meat comes from animals that led a natural life before they died.

Love grows things. Love and intimacy are as essential to the health and survival of human beings throughout their lives as food and shelter. Adults who live in satisfying relationships, who have work that fulfils them and who play a part in their community, are proven to be more likely to survive a whole range of ailments, from heart diseases and cancer to major surgery, than people who live in isolation.

Love says: you matter, you belong, you make a difference. Love gives my life meaning and tells me I am significant. Love weaves me into a bigger pattern. Love saves me from the fear of being lost.

In her garden my mother reads her plants. She knows where each one will flourish best, which needs tethering or propping up, which needs space and full sun to grow, which likes shade. She knows which is threatened by pests and which needs cutting back, and which will divide and create new plants to colonise empty corners. She knows because she loves her garden, and she pays it attention because she loves it, and so it loves her back. It grows. And in growing, it rewards her and she loves it all the more. I have learned, and maybe I learned it in my parents' garden, that where you see plants, animals, people flourish, then that is where love is.

Love and Sacrifice

What will you sacrifice for love? Your career? Your family? Your home? Your future? Your sex life? Your life? I don't think it is possible to get through life without sacrificing something for a greater good, particularly in a relationship.

Love begins by giving and ends by asking. At the discovery of a source of love in life I am so excited that I can only see the gift and not the price that may be asked. The price comes later, and there are many different prices because there are many different forms of love.

These are the prices I have paid for love in my life. I have paid the price of looking like a fool in pursuit of love. I have paid the price of losing my self-respect in pursuit of love. I have paid the price of abstinence and fidelity for the commitment of love. I have paid the price of leaving friends and family to follow love. I have paid the price of putting my career on the back-burner and losing my income to invest in love. I have paid the price of fatigue and loss of self in giving priority to love of family. I have paid the price of loss of independence and freedom for love of family. I have paid the price of loss of status in the world for love of family. I have paid the price of fatigue and loss of social life for love of music.

I have paid the price of fatigue and loss of income for love of art. I have paid, many times, the loss of freedom for love of those closest to me – even, and including, my cats. I have paid the price of loneliness for freedom and independence. And for each and every sacrifice I have felt it was worth it. Love repaid me with emotional richness, a calm conscience, a lack of regret, and an increased feeling of self-worth.

Self-denial and self-sacrifice are the prices exacted by love for the sake of something bigger than oneself. This bigger thing could be a partnership, a family or a community. It could be a country or a discipline or a cause. The worth of this price is increased if it is paid with cheerfulness and generosity, something I admit I don't always manage. I know that nobody loves a martyr. And nobody loves a masochist either. Nobody will thank you for sacrificing your career for their sake if you keep reminding them of what you've given up. Be careful you don't sacrifice the one and still lose the other.

What I have learned is that when you are young and longing to do and have everything, the idea of denial and self-sacrifice is unimaginable and, worse, old fashioned. But as the time comes for choice, if love demands it, the choice should be clear.

Beware, though, of pseudo-love that tries to control another by forcing them into sacrifices they needn't make. Beware of sacrificing yourself to another's jealousy rather than the higher good of the relationship. Insecure people often expect the ones they love to abandon anything that might exclude them: friends, sports, working life, even family. It is very dangerous to enter into a relationship with somebody so consuming that they demand the sacrifice of everything. Love exacts sacrifice for a higher good. If someone wants you to give up everything for them, it isn't love that's asking, it's the insatiable human ego.

A Day in the Life of My Father

I woke my father by entering his room quietly and drawing the curtains on to a dark January day. His head lay on its pillows, eyes closed, mouth slightly open. His thin body, once muscular and golden brown, scarcely made a mound beneath the covers. "Dad," I said gently, standing by his bedside, ready for the long business of helping him rise from bed and make his way to the bathroom on his Zimmer frame, waiting on the landing in case he fell.

That day I would help him to dress, easing his arms into a sweater as he winced and cried out with arthritic pain. I would follow as he went slowly downstairs, bring him his breakfast on a tray, his pills measured out into a glass. When he became exhausted by the effort of sitting upright and eating, I would help him very slowly up the stairs again, pulling back his bedcovers so that he could lie down, white and tired, and be warmly covered and left to sleep.

That day I helped him to wash. I put a chair by the washbasin and took a sponge and gently washed my father's back where the skin stretched tightly over the visible bones, feeling like the miners' wives who scrubbed their blackened husbands' work-worn bodies before the fire. But it wasn't mining that had wasted my father's body, it was tuberculosis.

I took the sponge and I squeezed it over my father's head, washing the soft white curls that were what was left of a head of thick, springing blond ringlets which had always been hard to control. I rubbed and dried and fluffed his hair with a towel, remembering how he had sometimes dried my hair with a towel when I was a child, and how he was rougher and stronger than my mother and how I loved the roughness.

In the evening I brought out the foot spa that my daughters had given him for Christmas, and I filled it with warm water and took off his socks and lifted his sore feet into the water. Relaxation softened his face and his body as the warm bubbles soothed his feet. I knelt and dried his feet with a towel, and then I took foot cream and massaged his dry feet with the cream until it was absorbed, feeling the pleasure of the intimate act, both physical and spiritual, of washing and caring for another's feet. My father loved this moment of the day.

At night I helped my father, drooped with the fatigue of the day and his illness, out of his day clothes, easing him out of his vest. I tucked a hot-water bottle between his sheets. I helped him lift and straighten his legs. I pulled up the sheets and duvet under his chin. I leaned down and kissed his forehead, feeling the skull beneath the skin.

"Who would have thought that one day I would be tucking you up into bed," I said, and I kissed him again. He kissed me back. I turned out his light and left him to sleep.

Sweet Mystery of Love

I end where I began, with a mystery. This is the one thing I know. It might even be the only thing I know for sure. Love is a mystery. We can observe its workings and try to fathom the laws of its physics, but in the end it is beyond our absolute control. Why I fall for that man is a mystery. And if he returns my love, or is indifferent, that is a mystery too. I can, and have, read many books of psychology and philosophy and biology and social history, and I can see that there are many actions I could take that would encourage the growth of love, but I can never guarantee the results.

I can congratulate myself smugly when the course of true love runs smooth – what do poets know? But I have no answers when, inexplicably, it turns a bit rough. I can wash that man right out of my hair until I am as bald as a coot, but the hair is gone and the man refuses to shift, dammit.

I can understand why I might be attracted to people and situations that replicate my childhood or remind me of my father, but I will still be baffled when I carefully and cleverly avoid that pitfall and head right down into another pitfall I hadn't even seen.

I learn, again and again, that love isn't all you need at all. You need patience and practice and perceptiveness and cleverness and resourcefulness, even ruthlessness and cunning. And you need a whole world of other consolations and fulfilments for when love in its songbook, cinematic, operatic guise has switched off its lights and gone off into the dark.

But without the mystery, where would be the ecstasy? Isn't that why one of the most powerful sensations that thrums in our hearts at the dawn of a new love is intoxicating disbelief? Whether you've just realised that your best friend was the love of your life all along, or whether some exotic piece of plotting by life has thrown an amazing stranger your way, can you believe love has really happened to you?

And mystery flows deeper than romance. I watched the pulse of my dying grandmother's heart beating insistently against her hundred-year-old ribs, as strong as the day she was born, and that was a profound mystery. And I've held my newborn children against my own heart and wondered who they were, and that was the greatest mystery of all. Their fingernails and eyelashes were mysterious, and so was the extraordinary piece of cosmic mathematics that brought me together with the man who was their father and produced these two miraculous creatures. Why him? Why me? Why them? Why love? Really, in the face of this mystery, all I can feel, despite the knowledge of grief and separation and heartache, despite the eclipse that throws its deep shadow in love's absence, is gratitude and awe that love came my way.

Love – the Conclusion

How do I feel now I've reached the end of writing down everything I've ever learned about love?

The first thing I feel is that this is not the end at all, although it may be the end of this particular book. Every day, while my thoughts have been focused on love, I have made some new connection. The antennae that twitch ceaselessly when you have a focus in life have been picking up signals wherever I go, presenting me with fresh questions and stimulating new insights.

I see love in the garden someone has made in a dark corner by the railway line. I see love in the face of a friend who is watching the little birds feed outside his window. I see love in the shrieks and embraces of teenage girls meeting one another for a night on the town. I see love in the habitual, forgiving pat that my mother's hand gives my father's hand. I could fill pages with these images and what they make me think and understand. Wait a minute. I already have.

It isn't all mushy and heart-warming, this love business – far from it. Its contemplation can stir great clouds of fear and loneliness from the depths. Its practice can take your breath away with the fear of losing control. It has been very challenging for me, Lesley, a woman in late middle age, to spend so much time in love's contemplation. It is all very well gaining a deeper understanding of the workings of love in a human life when, at the day and the book's end, I am alone.

But I am not alone in being alone, and that is a comfort and an encouragement. Millions of us are alone, more and more, especially women. The simple statistical fact is that we are all living longer. Broken relationships turn millions back on their own resources, and the patterns of the past are of little help. History and literature present us with models of life in couples and families, at a time when contemporary demography faces more and more of us with the challenge of making a meaningful and happy life outside these traditional patterns.

I wrote a story in my last book, *Everything I've Ever Done That Worked*, about receiving a mysterious message in the middle of a deserted park. The message, written on a piece of brown card stuck in a stick, said simply, "B Glad Your Free" – be glad you're free. It was a jolt and an inspiration then, when I applied it to my working life; and it is a jolt and an inspiration now when I apply it to my emotional life. If I turn my attention from loss to blessing, I am glad I'm free. The very notion lifts the sense of inner pressure and anxiety. Freedom is exhilarating and full of possibility.

I know that human beings are infinitely resilient and adaptable, and that we need one another. Love blocked in one direction finds fresh channels in which to flow, if we let it. Alone doesn't mean lonely, although it does mean you have to make more effort. It does mean taking responsibility for making our own lives work the way we would like them. It is often the broken places in our lives that make us resourceful and strong and send us spinning in a new direction.

My mother's oldest friend once told me that because she and her husband had never had children they had invested far more in friendship. That woman is now in her eighties and a widow, but when she was recently in hospital I couldn't visit her without finding at least half a dozen people at her bedside. Wherever she was it was party time.

My mother and my father have had a long, close marriage but fewer friends They are loved by the people who know them, but in comparison with their childless friends their social circle is smaller. Because they had each other, and they had me, they haven't invested in a wider world in the same way. I don't know if my mother's friend still regrets not having children, but by turning her attention outwards she leads a life in constant contact with loving friends and family of all ages, and she inspires us all.

Here I am, a long way from my eighties but far from my twenties too. I know that my views on love and connection are coloured by my age and the perspective it gives me. In my teens I would get in a turmoil about whether people liked or loved me. In my twenties I would drop everything for a likely boyfriend. Marriage and children absorbed me in my thirties and forties, and I know I made a lot of mistakes. Now that my own children are in their twenties I like the way that they and their friends give friendship such high value and aren't prepared to erase themselves in the pursuit of love. And I am single myself, and much more conscious of the ebb and flow of love and the many forms it takes.

And I know that it is still the highest value in a human life. I shall think about it and seek it till the day I die.

I was sitting in my favourite field today, listening to the cows munching and puffing, and I watched fat white clouds speed away eastwards. I could smell September approaching and the end of summer in the air. My eyes were caught by the reddening of hawthorn berries in the hedgerows, the dark bloom of sloes and the pale globes of hazelnuts. I felt my scratchy thoughts unravel and drift peacefully away, as they always do in this field that I love, where I can watch cloud shadows float on the far side of the valley.

Then my ear was caught by a mass of sudden twittering. I looked up and saw a swallow swooping by, and then more and more swallows. The swallows had been very active lately, sailing and looping by my high windows, and I realised that they would soon be gone. The sun was leaving, and the sun was calling them to Africa.

The sun is the gravity that pulls the swallows south, and love is the gravity that pulls us forward, if we let it. Even when it seems to have left my life I can see it warming other people, people who are temporarily more blessed. In cold dark moments it is easy to believe that love has gone forever, but I know it has just moved beyond the horizon.

If the swallows refused to believe the elemental pull of the sun as it moves away towards the tropics in winter, they would be stranded here. They would freeze and die. And if people refuse to believe in the continuing existence of love when it moves away from them, then they are in danger of freezing and dying too. Love is always there somewhere, just as the sun is.

I know that it is not the absence and withdrawal of love that is dangerous to me, it is the loss of faith. I may have to look for love in a different form. I may have to commit myself to being loving when I don't feel like it, or to give love doggedly when I don't feel it coming back, but this is what I must do. I must keep on engaging with life. It is a biological and a spiritual imperative. If I withdraw from love because I think it has withdrawn from me, I only deepen the darkness. The way to keep your heart alive is to express love in every way you think you can. Do the work and you prepare the ground for grace. And if redemption doesn't come your way, although I believe it will, you may still be the channel for it to come to someone else. That is the way love works.

Reading and Resource List

Thank you to Faber and Faber for permission to quote from Gwen Raverat's memoir, *Period Piece.*

For an unromantic but enlightening understanding of the chemistry of love and how it makes us all mad, I recommend *Love Sick, Love as a Mental Illness*, by Dr Frank Tallis, published by Century.

The two courses I recommend in "Fatal Loyalty" are the Orders of Love and the Hoffman Quadrinity Process.

For more information on Orders of Love or constellation work, look on the websites www.constellations.co.uk and www.ordersoflove.co.uk. They give a brief history of Bert Hellinger's work and information on forthcoming workshops.

The Hoffman Institute, at www.hoffmaninstitute.co.uk, regularly runs processes round the country and abroad. Tim Laurence's book, *You Can Change Your Life*, also gives a clear account of the process developed by Bob Hoffman and the thinking behind it. It is a very good introduction to the process but no substitute for doing it. It is published by Hodder Mobius.

The couples work of Maurice Taylor and Seanna McGee is fully explained in their book, *The New Couple: Why the old rules don't work and what does*. It is published by Harper San Francisco and contains a thorough explanation of the Peace Process outlined in "Love and Peace". For more details about their lectures and seminars look on their website, www.newcouple.com.

Thich Nhat Hanh's Peace Treaty is printed in full in his book *Teachings on Love*, published by Element.

I recommend very few books on love, since so many of them are formulaic and offer you glib rules to fix your love life. There is more to love than that. If you want to read more deeply, then I suggest you turn to the tried and tested spiritual teachings of the great religions, from Christianity to Buddhism. Poets do it best – and most succinctly – and it is a core theme of great fiction and drama. You will learn far more about love and human nature from seeing a Greek tragedy or a

Shakespeare play than you will from buying the latest marketing strategy to bag a partner. Love is what happens when being in love fades, which is why I also recommend Erich Fromm's thoughtful classic, *The Art of Loving*, published by Thorsons. He shows clearly how love is a practice, not a prize. For the same reason, I recommend Thich Nhat Hanh's book, *Teachings on Love*, mentioned above.

Everything I've Ever Learned about Change

If you enjoyed this book, you may also like Lesley Garner's new collection of essays, *Everything I've Ever Learned about Change* - a perfect bedside companion to her first two titles. She writes:

'Change is inevitable. Nothing stays still. From the molecular to the planetary level, life is in constant motion and we are changing right along with it. The Universe moves in a perpetual surging dance and happiness is the elation that comes from feeling in harmony with this cosmic rhythm.

'So why is change the source of so much fear and unhappiness? Why do we resist it so deeply and struggle against it so desperately? Why, if change is the norm, do we all recognise the profound, exhausted longing for eternal sameness? "Change and decay in all around I see," sing the mourners, "Oh Thou that changeth not, abide with me!"

'But if we could arrest change and enter a world of eternal stasis, we would come bang up against the great paradox. We would go mad quite quickly. Change is life. Stuckness is death. Constant adaptation creates the momentum and energy that keep us going. Our relationship with, and our understanding of, the forces of change within us and around us, the personal and the political, are crucial to our well-being. Without some surrender to change and understanding of its role in our life, we die.

'Life gives us endless chances to learn and practise. One minute life is stuck, the next minute life is out of control and moving at headlong speed. When life is stuck, we long to make changes. When life is out of control, we long for things to stay the same. If we can stay aware, we notice that there are two kinds of change: there are the changes that happen to us and there are the changes that we make happen. It is very important to understand the difference. The more of the second kind there is in our life, the happier we will be, but the art of dealing with change when it happens to us is also essential to happiness.

'Any human life is a never-ending lesson in adjusting to change: biological, hormonal, familial, changes of home or relationship, changes of mind and heart, changes of fortune and circumstance, changes of government and climate. A single life can encompass peaceful democracy and war, a perfect sunny day or a hurricane, the slow morphing of evolution or the cataclysm of a tsunami. The changes of life can flatten you or teach you to be skilfully adaptable, resourceful and even triumphant.

'So what can we do? We can do a lot. We can understand the forces that affect us and be better prepared. We can learn to read the writing on the wall, in relationships, in workplaces, in nations. We can learn and practise the arts of adaptation, self-preservation and creative living. We can learn how to nourish ourselves and anchor ourselves in those aspects of life which change more slowly than we do and give us glimpses of the eternal. And we can learn the empowerment that comes from being an agent of change. Change isn't something we have to suffer. It can be something we work to bring about.'

In *Everything I've Ever Learned about Change* Lesley Garner gives you techniques for dealing with change, some drawn from her own life, some from the experience and skills of others. Whether you are desperately stuck in the mud or being swept away in the current of life, this beautiful collection of essays will provide you with wonderful ideas that will get you riding the inevitable, interminable waves - ideas that will even have you enjoying a thrilling ride.

Everything I've Ever Learned About Change is available from all good bookshops, priced £10.00. Lesley's first book *Everything I've Ever Done That Worked* is also available from all good bookshops, priced £7.99. Alternatively, you can order both books direct from Hay House Publishers on 020 8962 1230.

We hope you enjoyed this Hay House book.
If you would like to receive a free catalogue featuring additional
Hay House books and products, or if you would like information
about the Hay Foundation, please contact:

Hay House UK Ltd
292B Kensal Rd • London W10 5BE
Tel: (44) 20 8962 1230; Fax: (44) 20 8962 1239
www.hayhouse.co.uk

***

Published and distributed in the United States of America by:
Hay House, Inc. • PO Box 5100 • Carlsbad, CA 92018-5100
Tel.: (1) 760 431 7695 or (1) 800 654 5126;
Fax: (1) 760 431 6948 or (1) 800 650 5115
www.hayhouse.com

Published and distributed in Australia by:
Hay House Australia Ltd • 18/36 Ralph St • Alexandria NSW 2015
Tel.: (61) 2 9669 4299; Fax: (61) 2 9669 4144
www.hayhouse.com.au

Published and distributed in the Republic of South Africa by:
Hay House SA (Pty) Ltd • PO Box 990 • Witkoppen 2068
Tel./Fax: (27) 11 706 6612 • orders@psdprom.co.za

Published and distributed in India by:
Hay House Publishers India • Muskaan Complex • Plot No.3
B-2 • Vasant Kunj • New Delhi – 110 070.
Tel.: (91) 11 41761620; Fax: (91) 11 41761630.
contact@hayhouseindia.co.in

Distributed in Canada by:
Raincoast • 9050 Shaughnessy St • Vancouver, BC V6P 6E5
Tel.: (1) 604 323 7100; Fax: (1) 604 323 2600

***

Sign up via the Hay House UK website to receive the Hay House
online newsletter and stay informed about what's going on with
your favourite authors. You'll receive bimonthly announcements
about discounts and offers, special events, product highlights,
free excerpts, giveaways, and more!
www.hayhouse.co.uk